PLEC

D0085347

WOMEN AND UTOPIA

Critical Interpretations

WITHDRAWN

Edited by

Marleen Barr
Nicholas D. Smith
Virginia Polytechnic Institute and State University

UNIVERSITY
PRESS OF
AMERICA

LANHAM • NEW YORK • LONDON

Copyright © 1983 by

University Press of America,™ Inc.

4720 Boston Way
Lanham, MD 20706

3 Henrietta Street
London WC2E 8LU England

All rights reserved
Printed in the United States of America

Library of Congress Cataloging in Publication Data

Main entry under title:

Women and utopia.

Includes bibliographical references.
1. American fiction—History and criticism—Addresses,
essays, lectures. 2. Utopias in literature—Addresses,
essays, lectures. 3. American fiction—Women authors—
History and criticism—Addresses, essays, lectures.
4. Women in literature—Addresses, essays, lectures.
5. Sex role in literature—Addresses, essays, lectures.
6. Feminism and literature—Addresses, essays, lectures.
7. Lessing, Doris May, 1919-   —Criticism and
interpretation—Addresses, essays, lectures. I. Barr,
Marleen S. II. Smith, Nicholas D.
PS374.U8W65   1984   813'.009'372   83-16920
ISBN 0-8191-3558-5 (alk. paper)
ISBN 0-8191-3559-3 (pbk. : alk. paper)

All University Press of America books are produced on acid-free
paper which exceeds the minimum standards set by the National
Historical Publications and Records Commission.

CA [Ma, 19 '86

SSS English

4-28-86 mls 25.88

WOMEN AND UTOPIA: CRITICAL INTERPRETATIONS

ALLEGHENY COLLEGE LIBRARY

85-6956

To Ann and Art Eastman

ACKNOWLEDGEMENT

The production of this book was made possible by the computer resources of Virginia Polytechnic Institute and State University. We wish to thank the English and Philosophy departments for making computer time available to us.

NOTE

Because of computer formatting, the spacing between words, ellipses, and hyphens is sometimes irregular.

CONTENTS

PREFACE

    People write and read utopian fiction for a
variety of reasons. Such fiction can provide social
criticism and satire, visionary speculation, moral
prescriptions, even light fantasy, depending upon the
wit, will and skill of the author, and the perception
and participation of the reader.
    For a fictive vision to qualify as utopian,
however, it must at least apply to, if not directly
concern itself with, the institutions and interactions
of persons. Such persons need not be human, as a
number of science fiction works might well be argued to
be utopian even though treating alien cultures. But
typically utopia is conceived as a human place, and
certainly a humane place, and where aliens are
portrayed as inhabiting this place, we might well
expect to see in them the perfection of humanity,
broadly conceived. To conceive of utopia, then, is
from the outset to reconstruct human culture. Many of
the most fundamental elements of human nature as we
know it derive from the fact that we are sexed
creatures -- herein lie many of our hopes and
frustrations, our goals and fantasies, even our
conceptions of ourselves. Just as importantly,
however, sexual differences are expressed throughout
our institutions -- indeed, too often this expression
has little or no natural basis in human sexual biology,
but is rather the product of social conventions that
are increasingly (and with good reason) being
scrutinized for their social, political, and moral
consequences.
    In this book, we offer essays that address issues
in the ways in which the female, and sex roles in
general, are portrayed in utopian fiction. Some, but
not all of these essays are feminist in approach; some,
but not all are written by women; some, but not all of
the utopian works cited within these essays are written
by, specifically about, or for women. All of these
essays, however, concern themselves with an essential

part of our culture, and its aspect in utopia, that is of surpassing influence on our lives and consciousnesses. Just as there are women, as distinct from men, there are institutions that represent this fact. Should there be such institutions at all? If so, which? If not, which may be eliminated as invalid? Utopian fiction often pursues these questions in a particularly appealing and vivid way, and these essays allow us to follow this pursuit with even greater clarity and care. Herein, therefore, are offered some of our hopes and our fears, our dreams and our plans, for women in utopia.

Marleen Barr   Nicholas D. Smith

A NEW ANARCHISM:
SOCIAL AND POLITICAL IDEAS IN SOME RECENT FEMINIST EUTOPIAS

Lyman Tower Sargent

The utopian novel has been used to depict almost every imaginable form of social organization plus a few that are a bit hard to imagine. The form that has appeared the fewest times is anarchism. There have been works that most people would call anarchist -- such as Robert Blatchford's *The Sorcery Shop* (1907) and William Morris's *News from Nowhere* (1890) (Morris vehemently rejected the label) -- but almost every other form has appeared many more times.
    In recent years, though, there have been a number of writers, mostly women, who have written anarchist eutopias (good places) and even labeled them as such. Alternatively, one could say that a number of eutopias have been published normally labeled feminist which, on examination, turn out to share an outlook on social organization that can be called anarchist.
    There are a couple of problems regarding anarchism which stand in the way of understanding this new phenomenon. One problem is that both popular and scholarly images of anarchism often misrepresent it. The anarchist symbol should not be that which is usually evoked -- a man in a long, black beard holding a bomb behind his back. In fact, according to the recent eutopias, a man as the symbol of anarchism is wrong. Men are given to authority and hierarchy as well as patriarchy. Women, being given to freedom and equality, are most likely to be anarchists; therefore, a woman should be the symbol of anarchism.
    A second misunderstanding of anarchism (closely related to the previous one and the woman symbol) is the common belief that anarchism rejects cooperation in favor of the isolated, independent individual. Nothing could be further from the truth.

Lyman Tower Sargent

Of course, there are a variety of anarchisms; a brand of individualist anarchism associated with Max Stirner (1806-1856) and contemporary capitalist anarchism looks something like the usual conception. But most anarchism stresses cooperation among individuals rather than isolated independence.

The Variety of Anarchisms[1]

In order to understand the anarchist thinking represented in the novels to be considered, it is necessary to know something about the traditions of anarchist thought and the recent changes which have taken place in anarchism even though the novelists are only rarely responding to anarchism as developed by any specific thinker or group of thinkers. There is one exception (Ursula K. Le Guin), but the exception does not make any serious difference to the point that generally the novelists do not think of themselves as participating in an anarchist dialogue. At the same time, even though they do not so conceive themselves, they now are part of such a dialogue just because their ideas so closely resemble developments in anarchist thought.
     These novelists (I have chosen to limit my consideration to the women writers) reflect currents of thought, fairly common in the 1960s and 70s, which represented something of a change in anarchist thinking. (Perhaps it would be more accurate to say that the novels reflect aspects of New Left thinking

----

[1]For general studies of anarchism in English, see April Carter, *The Political Theory of Anarchism*. London: Routledge & Kegan Paul, 1971; James Joll, *The Anarchists*. 2nd ed. London: Methuen, 1979; Alan Ritter, *Anarchism: A Theoretical Analysis*. Cambridge: Cambridge University Press, 1980; and George Woodcock, *Anarchism: A History of Libertarian Ideas and Movements*. Cleveland: World Pub. Co., 1982. This section is based on the chapter "Anarchism" in Lyman Tower Sargent, *Contemporary Political Ideologies: A Comparative Analysis*. 5th ed. (Homewood, IL: The Dorsey Press, 1981), pp. 148-165.

which have also been reflected in anarchist thought.)
Many anarchists deny there was such a change, but while
it is possible to argue about the extent of the change,
there is no question but that there has been a change.
Today, the changes are less obvious than they were a
few years ago because most anarchism has absorbed the
lessons of the 60s and 70s.
Peter Kropotkin (1824-1921), probably the greatest
anarchist thinker, defined anarchism as follows:

> . . .the name given to a principle or
> theory of life and conduct under which
> society is conceived without government --
> harmony in such a society being obtained,
> not by submission to law or by obedience
> to any authority, but by free agreements
> concluded between the various groups,
> territorial and professional, freely
> constituted for the sake of production and
> consumption, as also for the satisfaction
> of the infinite variety of needs and
> aspirations of a civilized being.[2]

To the extent there is an agreed definition of

----

[2]Peter Kropotkin, "Anarchism," *Encyclopedia Britannica*,
11th ed., vol. 1, p. 914.
A sampling of definitions follows: "The basic
anarchist vision is one of a society where all
relationships are those of social and economic equals
who act together in voluntary cooperation for material
benefit." Robert Hoffman (ed.) *Anarchism* (New York:
Atherton Press, 1970), p. 9.
"Anarchism: The philosophy of a new social order
based on liberty unrestricted by man-made law; the
theory that all forms of government rest on violence,
and are therefore wrong and harmful, as well as
unnecessary." Emma Goldman, *Anarchism and Other Essays*
(New York: Dover, 1969), p. 50. Originally published
as 3rd rev. ed. 1917.
"The fundamental idea that man is by nature good
and that it is institutions that corrupt him remains
the basis of all anarchist thought. . . ." James Joll,
The Anarchists (London: Eyre & Spottiswoode, 1964), p.
30.

anarchism, this is it. Anarchism is a political philosophy contending that no one (individual or group) should hold coercive authority. This principle is rooted in certain hypotheses about the effect of coercion on the human psyche and human behavior. On a simple level, the contention is that coercion breeds coercion and that, conversely, freedom breeds freedom. The statement is not left at that level but is developed into a coherent vision of both how human beings ought to interact with each other and what the positive results of such noncoercive interaction will be.

According to anarchism, most of our problems arise because we allow ourselves and others to be controlled rather than controlling our own lives and letting others control theirs. "Many people say government is necessary because some men cannot be trusted to look after themselves, but anarchists say that government is harmful because no man can be trusted to look after anyone else."[3] Anarchists extend this condemnation of political power deeply into social and economic relationships. No person should be in a position to force or coerce another be that person a teacher, manager, wife, husband or parent.

"This was the bond that united all anarchists: antagonism to any situation regulated by imposition, constraint, or oppression." Roderick Kedward, *The Anarchists: The Men Who Shocked an Era* (Somerset, Eng.: Purnell & Sons, 1971), p. 6.

"When anarchism in its several forms, including its theoretical statements and practical experiments, is analyzed structurally, it generally separates into three broad areas of tactics and strategy: (a) a rejection of constituted authority as the source of social dynamism and equilibrium; (b) a refusal to collaborate with the existing order anywhere through participation in any program of reformism; (c) the promotion of a variety of noncoercive alternatives of quite clearly defined nature as a substitute." James J. Martin, *Men Against the State:the Expositors of Individualistic Anarchism in America,1827-1908* (Colorado Springs, Co.: Ralph Myles, 1970), p. vii. Originally published 1953.

"If there is any unity at all to be found among the anarchists it is in their common antipathy to

This does not mean that society will be a totally unorganized group of isolated individuals. Society can exist, anarchists contend, without power and authority. Society cannot only exist; it can thrive. "Given a common need, a collection of people will, by trial and error, by improvisation and experiment, evolve order out of the chaos -- this order being more durable than any kind of externally imposed order."[4] This order must not be coercive; it must be "(1) voluntary, (2) functional, (3) temporary, and (4) small."[5]

The ethos of anarchism is thus a combination of the rejecting of coercion and the affirmation of the possibilities of voluntary cooperation. Anarchism is too often seen solely as a strong negation of authority. It has a positive side which is at least as important.

Within anarchism there are two basic tendencies which can be labeled collectivist and individualist. Collectivist anarchism is the best known and the most developed as a theory. Individualist anarchism is a permanent minority position within anarchism, although it has recently become more popular in the United States as what can be called anarcho-capitalism. Most U.S. anarcho-capitalists have, at some point, been followers of Ayn Rand.[6]

----

political order (whether established or disestablished) and their concomitant dedication not merely to the eventual achievement of radical alternatives, but to the necessity for a revolutionary (though not always violent or cataclysmic) overthrow of present order to reach their goals. Anarchism is, then, a doctrine of revolution, and anarchists are always rebels (whatever else they may be)." Benjamin R. Barber, *Superman and Common Men: Freedom, Anarchy, and the Revolution* (New York: Praeger, 1971), p. 16.
[3]Nicolas Walter, *About Anarchism* (London: Freedom Press, 1969), p. 6. Originally published as *Anarchy 100*, 9 (June 1969).
[4]Colin Ward, "Anarchism as a Theory of Organization," *Anarchy 62*, 6 (April 1966), p. 103.
[5]Ibid., p. 101. See also Terry Phillips, "Organization -- The Way Forward," *Freedom*, 31 (August 22, 1972), p. 3.
[6]See Jerome Tuccille, *It Usually Begins with Ayn Rand*.

Lyman Tower Sargent

Collectivist anarchism argues that communities of
individuals will be formed for mutual benefit, with
people cooperating to help each other. Individualist
anarchism stresses competition as the major basis for
human interaction. All the novelists considered use of
the collectivist form.
Recently, there has been a growing emphasis within
anarchism on what might be called the non-rational side
of human life as opposed to the reasoning or rational
side, which has traditionally been emphasized. There
is, as mentioned earlier, some dispute over whether or
not this is a new emphasis or enough of a change to
argue that there has been a split.[7] There has certainly
been enough change to talk about a new anarchism more
concerned with affective than economic relationships
or, to use slightly different terminology, with
reproductive or nurturant rather than productive
relationships.
Anarchism has always recognized that life is not
limited to the economic and political. According to
anarchists (and most thinking human beings) sex, family
life, education, friendship and so forth are at least
as, and probably more, important. Commentators, mostly
not anarchists, have tended to ignore this fact;

New York: Stein and Day, 1971.
[7]The most explicit case of the controversy can be found
in the differences between the first and second series
of the British journal *Anarchy*. The following give an
idea of the approaches. Most important is Guy Debord,
La Societe du Spectacle. Paris: Buchet Chastel, 1971;
unauthorized translation, Detroit: Black and Red, 1973.
See also *Anarchy*, 2nd series, and Broadstreet (Sydney
Libertarians) for different examples of the periodical
literature. In addition, see Christopher Gray, ed.
and trans., *The Incomplete Work of the Situationist
International.* London: Free Fall Publications, 1974;
Rudolf de Jong, *Provos and Kabouters*. Buffalo, N.Y.:
Friends of Malatesta, n.d.; *Hip Culture*. New York:
Times Change Press, 1970; Jeff Nuttall, *Bomb Culture*.
London: Paladin, 1968; Peter Stansill and David Zane
Mairowitz, eds., *Bamn*. Harmondsworth, England:
Penguin, 1971; *Surrealism and Revolution*. London: Wooden
Shoe, n.d.; Roel Van Duyn, *Message of a Wise Kabouter*,
trans. Hubert Hoskins. London: Duckworth, 1969; Raoul

therefore, anarchism, accurately depicted, would include this wider sphere of activity. But the major anarchist figures, identified as such by both anarchists and non-anarchist commentators, have stressed the productive spheres of life. Thus, there has been a shift of emphasis. In addition, there has been a rejection of reason as the sole route to the problem solving. This is a clear repudiation of much of the anarchist past.

Today, there has been a reconciliation. Reasoning and the nonrational are being recombined into a more comprehensive whole. Anarchists of all collectivist stripes are fully aware that both productive and reproductive activites are essential. All the novelists presenting anarchist societies make this point clearly.

Ursula K. Le Guin[8]

The writer who most clearly related her ideas (at least as presented in her most explicitly political work) to anarchism is Ursula K. Le Guin. Her *The Dispossessed*

Vaneigem, *The Revolution of Everyday Life*, trans. John Fullerton and Paul Sieveking. London: Practical Paradise Publications, 1975; and *The Veritable Split in the International*. London: Harpo Press, 1974. The most sustained rejection of the thesis that there is a "new" anarchism can be found in Nicolas Walter, "Has Anarchism Changed?" *Freedom's Anarchist Review* 37 (April 17, 1976), pp. 9-10; (May 1, 1976), pp. 11-12; (June 26, 1976), pp. 9-10; (July 10, 1976), pp. 12-13.
[8]On Le Guin, see Barbara J. Bucknall, *Ursula K. Le Guin*. New York: Frederick Ungar, 1981; Joe De Bolt (ed.), *Ursula K. Le Guin: Voyager to Inner Lands and Outer Space*. Port Washington, N.Y.: Kennikat Press, 1979; Joseph D. Olander and Martin Harry Greenberg (eds.), *Ursula K. Le Guin*. New York: Taplinger, 1979; George Edgar Slusser, *The Farthest Shores of Ursula K. Le Guin*. San Bernardino, Calif.: Borgo Press, 1976; Rosemarie Arbur, "Beyond Feminism, the Self Interest: Women's Place in the Work of Ursula K. Le Guin," in *Selected Proceedings of the 1978 Science Fiction Research Association Conference*, ed. Thomas J.

Lyman Tower Sargent

(1974)[9] is certainly the work of science fiction best
known to students of political thought. *The
Dispossessed* is an anarchist eutopia (good place) and
shows considerable sophistication in illustrating the
ways in which such a society might change over time and
what problems might develop.

Sometimes it seems as if Le Guin's emphasis is on
the problems rather than the successes, but a balance
is achieved. Still, the subtitle of the book -- *An
Ambiguous Utopia* -- must be stressed. *The Dispossessed*
does not present a perfect world inhabited by perfect
people but a harsh, cruel, unforgiving world peopled by
real human beings with all their faults.

Annares, the anarchist society, does not have any
government in our sense. As the main character,
Shevek, says, "'The network of administration and
management is called PDC, Production and Distribution
Coordination. They are a coordinating system for all
syndicates, federatives, and individuals that do
productive work. They do not govern persons; they
administer production. They have no authority either
to support me or to prevent me. They can only tell us
the public opinion of us -- where we stand in the
social conscience'" (p. 67). But there are problems.

Remington (Cedar Falls: University of Northern Iowa,
1979), pp. 146-163; Dena C. Bain, "The *Tao Ta Ching* as
Background to the Novels of Ursula K. Le Guin,"
Extrapolation, 21, No. 3 (Fall 1980), pp. 209-222;
Marleen S. Barr, "Charles Bronson, Samurai, and Other
Feminine Images: A Transactive Response to *The Left
Hand of Darkness*," in *Future Females: A Critical Anthology*,
ed. Marleen S. Barr (Bowling Green, O.: Bowling Green
State University Popular Press, 1981), pp. 138-154;
Judah Bierman, "Ambiguity in Utopia: The
Dispossessed," *Science-Fiction Studies*, 2 (November 1975),
pp. 249-255; Barbara Brown, "The Left Hand of Darkness:
Androgyny, Future,. Present, and Past," *Extrapolation*, 21,
No. 3 (Fall 1980), pp. 227-235; Leonard M. Fleck,
"Science Fiction as a Tool of Speculative Philosophy: A
Philosophical Analysis of Selected Anarchistic and
Utopian Themes in *The Dispossessed*," in *Selected
Proceedings*, pp. 133-145; John Huntington, "Public and
Private Imperatives in Le Guin's Novels," *Science-Fiction
Studies*, 2 (November 1975), pp. 237-142; Frederic

Public opinion becomes coercive. "'We've let cooperation become obedience'" (p. 146).[10] This does not mean violence or any direct coercion. As Shevek says, "'Coercion is the least efficient means of obtaining order'" (p. 131), but public opinion has established limits on acceptable behavior. One freely chooses to do what is expected and, thus, never questions whether or not some freedom has been lost.

In addition, Le Guin suggests that some people have begun to manipulate both public opinion and the various means of social decision making (from computers to committees that choose materials for publication) so that anyone different may have a difficult time. The favorite put-down is "Don't egoize!" which is used by some to reject anyone different or even unusually creative.

For all its problems Annares is still a good society. The first key to understanding how it works is decentralization.

> Decentralization had been an essential element in Odo's plans for the society she did not live to see founded. She had no intention to de-urbanize civilization.

Jameson, "World Reduction in Le Guin: The Emergence of Utopian Narrative," *Science-Fiction Studies*, 2 (November 1975), pp. 221-230; David J. Lake, "Le Guin's Twofold Vision: Contrary Image-Sets in *The Left Hand of Darkness*," *Science-Fiction Studies*, 8 (July 1981), pp. 156-164; Steven A. Peterson and Douglas Saxton, "Science Fiction and Political Thought: *The Dispossessed*," *Cornell Journal of Social Relations*, 12, No. 1 (Spring 1977), pp. 65-74; David L. Porter, "The Politics of Le Guin's Opus," *Science-Fiction Studies*, 2 (November 1975), pp. 243-248; Kathleen L. Spencer, "Exiles and Envoys: the SF of Ursula K. Le Guin," *Foundation*, No. 20 (October 1980), pp. 32-43; M. Teresa Tavormina, "Physics as Metaphor: The General Temporal Theory in *The Dispossessed*," *Mosaic*, 13, 3-4 (Spring-Summer 1980), pp. 51-62; Donald F. Theall, "The Art of Social-Science Fiction: The Ambiguous Dialectics of Ursula K. Le Guin," *Science-Fiction Studies*, 2 (November 1975), pp. 256-264; Victor Urbanowicz, "Personal and Political in *The Dispossessed*," *Science-Fiction Studies*, 5

Though she suggested that the natural
limit to the size of a community lay in
its dependence on its own immediate region
for essential food and power, she intended
that all communities be connected by
communication and transportation networks,
so that goods and ideas could get where
they were wanted, and the administration
of things might work with speed and ease,
and no community should be set off from
change and interchange. But the network
was not to run from the top down (pp.
83-84).

The economy of Annares is also based on free
cooperation and decentralization. Every individual
freely gives a day of community labor about every ten
days. Their approach to work is recognized as not the
most efficient but as humane, which is more important.
"Most Annarresti worked five to seven hours a day, with
two to four days off each decad. Details of
regularity, punctuality, which days off, and so on were
worked out between the individual and his work crew or
gang or syndicate or coordinating federative, on

(July 1978), pp. 110-117; Kingsley Widmer, "Utopian,
Dystopian, Diatopian Libertarianism: Le Guin's *The
Dispossessed*," *The Sphinx*, No. 13. vol. 4, No. 1 (1981),
pp. 55-66; and Susan Wood, "Discovering Worlds: The
Fiction of Ursula K. Le Guin," in *Voices for the Future*:
Essays on Major Science Fiction Writers, ed. Thomas D.
Clareson (Bowling Green,: Bowling Green University
Popular Press, 1979), vol. 2, pp. 154-179.
[9]Ursula K. Le Guin, *The Dispossessed*: *An Ambiguous Utopia*.
New York: Harper and Row, 1974. A story which forms
part of the background to *The Dispossessed* should also
be read -- "The Day Before the Revolution," in *Nebula
Award Stories Ten*, ed. James Gunn (New York: Harper and
Row, 1975), pp. 129-146. First published in *Galaxy*,
35, No. 8 (August 1974).
[10] Compare the analysis in Philip Slater, *The Pursuit of
Loneliness*: *American Culture at the Breaking Point*, rev. ed.
Boston: Beacon, 1976. Le Guin wrote one directly
coercive utopia. See, "The Diary of the Rose," in
Future Power, ed. Jack Dann and Gardner Dozois (New

A New Anarchism

whichever level cooperation and efficiency could be achieved" (P. 164). Clearly, such arrangements leave the door open to potential subtle coercion and such coercion did happen. But people volunteered for hard or dangerous jobs; no one was ever required to take a job they did not choose. And, of course, no one took a job they hated because they had to make a living.

All goods are distributed freely; everything is free to take at depositories. Again, public opinion is the major means of ensuring that the system is not abused. At least, that is the external form of social control; more important is the internal one. No one would think of abusing the system.

Education is designed to fit the needs of the society. The curriculum ". . . included farming, carpentry, sewage reclamation, printing, plumbing, roadmending, and all other occupations of the adult community. . ." (p. 130). Anyone with special talent is supposed to be helped to develop it. This normally worked, but sometimes the jealousy of an average person for the very talented posed problems.

Men and women are equal. This is neatly symbolized by the fact that the only verb to describe sexual intercourse takes a plural subject. "It meant something two people did, not something one person did or had" (p. 47). The greatest success of Anarres is found in the equality of the sexes; there were no failures here.

The Dispossessed is *An Ambiguous Utopia*; it presents a flawed[11] but highly desirable society. The flaws are human flaws, and they illustrate the problems an anarchist society must constantly fear and guard against.[12]

York: Random House, 1976), pp. 4-31.

[11]For another flawed utopia by Le Guin, see "The Ones Who Walk Away from Omelas (Variations on a Theme by William James)," in *New Dimensions 3*, ed. Robert Silverberg (Garden City: Nelson Doubleday, 1973), pp. 1-8.

[12]For a general discussion of this problem, see Lyman Tower Sargent, "Social Decision Making in Anarchism and Minimalism," *The Personalist*, 59, No. 4 (October 1978), pp. 358-369.

An earlier work, *The Left Hand of Darkness* (1969),[13] describes the planet Gethen (known to others as Winter) and two societies there. Gethen is interesting primarily because the sexual nature of the people allows Le Guin to raise questions about the influence of sexuality on personal psychology and social relations.

Gethenians are hermaphrodites who have a sexual cycle of twenty-six to twenty-eight days. During what they call *kemmer* (estrus), Gethenians take on male or female sexual characteristics. There is no predisposition to either sexual role and the sex role is only established in combination with another person in *kemmer*.

In one sense, their androgynous nature dominated Gethenian society; in another sense, sex is less important than it is to those who are in permanent *kemmer*. The Gethenians think of such people (us) as perverts. When not in *kemmer*, the Gethenian's normal state is one of mixed sexuality (woman/man, man/woman). Many social institutions and practices on Gethen are related to *kemmer*, but they consider this period of dominating sexuality as a normal part of a cycle and cannot understand how the duality of our sexuality can pervade society. For them the norm is to be asexual.

Thus, a Gethenian, while similar, is truly alien, and Le Guin explores the possibility of friendship between aliens. Friendship then becomes the strong political statement of the book and what brings *The Left Hand of Darkness* into this essay.

All government on Gethen is bad, whether the more or less constitutional monarchy of Karhide or the Soviet style Communism in Orgoreyn. Friendship and custom are the only positives in *The Left Hand of Darkness*. The customary law of the Domains of Karhide (the traditional social and political units) can produce strong, capable people who have a deep capacity for friendship and love.

The basic social unit is the Hearth, a kinship and geographical grouping. The harsh conditions of Gethen make hospitality the norm, but friendship, particularly friendship between aliens, is hard and is achieved only through struggle with oneself and one's socialization.

----

[13]*The Left Hand of Darkness*. New York: Walker, 1969.

The androgynous nature of Gethenians does not seem
to have much impact on their non-sexual behavior. Some
are good, strong, loving people and some are bad, weak,
and full of hate.

Since Le Guin makes the point that human female
and male are more alien to each other than Gethenian
and human, it is impossible to avoid seeing this tale
of hard-won friendship between aliens as an allegory on
human female-male friendship. Read this way, such
friendship is extremely difficult but possible and is
clearly more important than such minor obstructions as
law and government. The real basis for a decent
society is such friendship, and in this sense *The Left
Hand of Darkness* does at least imply that if one is to
have a eutopia, it must be an anarchist one.

Still, the sexual stereotyping of our culture
stands in the way of the understanding that is
necessary to achieve friendship. The sex roles that
become such an integral part of our behavior make a
better society almost impossible. At the same time,
the androgynous Gethenians have not produced a better
society either so Le Guin is not arguing for a new
androgyny as the way out. Her better society is the
flawed one of *The Dispossessed*.

A later work, "The Eye of the Heron" (1978),[14]
develops the anarchism of *The Dispossessed* by stressing
non-violence. In one sense, "The Eye of the Heron" is
not a eutopia. While it is certainly nowhere, it
includes a strongly realized, male chauvinist dystopia
(bad place). About fifty years apart, earth chose to
settle a planet with two groups of troublemakers who
could hardly be expected to cooperate. The first
colony was penal. Its members were mostly men. The
second colony, also founded as a punishment, was a
group of pacifists. The first established The City,
developed an authoritarian system which they believed
encompassed the second group. The lower class members
of the penal colony work rather poorly at some minor
industries, and they fish. The pacifists become
farmers, weavers, and artisans and effectively control

----

[14]"The Eye of the Heron," in *Millennial Women*, ed.
Virginia Kidd (New York: Delacorte Press, 1978), pp.
124-302. The novel was republished separately as *The
Eye of The Heron*. London: Panther, 1980.

ALLEGHENY COLLEGE LIBRARY

the economy of the planet without making a point of it and without the rather stupid male leaders of The City noticing what has happened.

The city is a male chauvinist dystopia. Women are the property of men and should never have a thought of their own. They are fragile commodities which must be protected so they can then be exploited. The Shantish (Shanty Town to The City) have developed an anarchical, egalitarian eutopia, although many members wish to wholly free themselves from the unwelcome attentions of The City. This provides the social drama of the novel.

The personal drama is provided by Luz Falco (daughter of The Boss of The City) who chooses the Shantish and hardship on a trek to a new area of the planet over her destined role as a wife in The City. She emerges as a strong leader.

Most of the novel focuses on the personal and social conflict involved and the tensions this produces in both dystopia and eutopia. The symbol of the eutopia is the fauna of the planet, all of which die if caged or confined in any way. This almost happened to the Shantish, but some of them managed to maintain their freedom and lived as human beings rather than caged animals.

Another novel, *The Word for World is Forest* (1972),[15] presents a world on which the inhabitants live in a complex, matriarchal society which is intimately part of the ecology of the planet. Men from earth are ruthlessly destroying the ecology and the society to provide wood for an earth now devoid of trees. The ensuing struggle may have destroyed some central, positive features of the native society; but it is still better than human society, though unfortunately, more like it. The natives have now learned, for the first time, how to kill.

The native society has few laws although there are taboos. The women are active; the men dream, a dreaming that is a creative part of life rather like that found in another of these eutopias, Dorothy Bryant's *The Kin of Ata are Waiting for You* (1976-1971 as

----

[15]*The Word for World is Forest*. New York: Berkley, 1976. Originally published in *Again, Dangerous Visions*, ed. Harlan Ellison (Garden City: Doubleday, 1972), pp. 32-117.

ALLEGHENY COLLEGE LIBRARY

The Comforter).[16]

Dorothy Bryant

The Kin of Ata are Waiting for You presents a physically harsh, primitive society which is spiritually and mentally advanced. Located somewhere on earth, Ata has an agricultural economy; since the people are very close to the animals and birds, they eat no meat. They tend their fields carefuly in patterns learned in their dreams.

Life in Ata is controlled by the dreams the people have. Names come in dreams, as do planting patterns and rituals. In fact, most important decisions are made through dreams.

Every morning each person tells another person his or her dreams of the night before. This is the first ritual of each day. The last ritual of the day is communal eating (no person feeds themselves but is fed by others) followed by storytelling. The whole system came from someone's dream. Even the stories were dreamed first and are now handed down through the generations.

Ata is anarchist; one follows one's dreams, and no one would consider objecting or suggesting otherwise. But healthy dreams come from a healthy life and unhealthy ones from an unhealthy life. Thus, the daily pattern of work and leisure which produces good dreams is essential to both individual and communal well-being.

A surface simplicity hides a richly complex life, but a life where no one directs, orders or coerces another. Children are raised communally in a loving atmosphere. Sex is chosen by two completely equal

----

[16]Originally published as Dorothy Bryant, *The Comforter*. Berkeley, Calif.: Moon Books, 1971. Edition used -- *The Kin of Ata are Waiting for You*. Berkeley Calif./New York: Moon Books/Random House, 1976. See Carol Pearson, "Beyond Governance: Anarchist Feminism in the Utopian Novels of Dorothy Bryant, Marge Piercy and Mary Staton," *Alternative Futures*, 4, No. 1 (Winter 1981), pp. 126-135.

people, and the relationship may last briefly (as it mostly does for the young) or (rarely) as long as a lifetime.

Ata is a eutopia; the mission of Ata is to keep the rest of the earth from going over the brink to destruction. To do this individuals from Ata choose (directed by their dreams) to sacrifice themselves by going to the dystopia which is our life until they gain the final release of death.

Mary Staton

Another of the anarchist utopias which presents us as dystopia is Mary Staton's *From the Legend of Biel* (1975).[17] She includes two eutopias (one a higher stage of the other) and one dystopia. The dystopia is our contemporary world projected approximately two hundred years into the future. This world is clearly an improvement on ours today, but within the context of the book it is a bad place producing narrow-minded, fearful, destructive people whose first instinct is to destroy what they don't understand.

The two eutopias are on a different time line on the planet which a scared earthman bombs (as a result one is left uncertain about his effect). The first eutopia is, in the word used by a member of the second, a "technocracy." The second eutopia has passed beyond complete dependence on machines to a fuller use of human potential. From our perspective, the first, technological eutopia, would be an incredible improvement: the second eutopia goes a few steps further.

From the Legend of Biel contains little description of either society. The technological eutopia is ultimately based on the realization that the syntax of our language (the deep meaning) often contradicted what the words seemed to say. They discovered what they call the syntax of despair. "Hidden deep in the sounds of their [our] words was despair and fear. Repeated use of the words and phrases only reinforced those

----

[17]Mary Staton, *From the Legend of Biel*. New York: Ace, 1975. See Pearson, "Beyond Governance."

A New Anarchism

feelings" (p. 176).
Our language says that we can own and control
everything.

> They [us] permitted governments and
> systems to try and control nonexistent
> entities like The People, Education,
> Health, even Death. They could not seem
> to understand that it is impossible to own
> mates, progeny, land, knowledge or
> emotions. States cannot control events.
> They cannot prevent change. They cannot
> be the stewards of The People because
> there is no such thing as The People.
> There are only persons" (p. 176).

But to some extent they have given authority to
technology specifically a large "computer," Thoacdien,
which or who makes most of the society's policy
decisions. Still, there are definite limits on
Thoacdien's ability to interfere with individuals.
Specifically, as long as no harm comes to another, each
person is free to do as he or she chooses.
At the same time, the society is "naturally
stratified" based on "experience, knowledge [and]
wisdom" (p. 172). There are four groups -- infants,
youth, peers, and elders. The entire society is
devoted to personal development and learning. Each
peer, for example, continues to learn with an elder
while acting as a mentor for a youth. The infants are
mostly taken care of by machines while they learn
enough to become youths.
While this is a caring society, Thoacdien seems
more interested in furthering the concerns and capacity
of the race than in individuals. There is no direct
conflict with Thoacdien, but the higher eutopia is
formed by people choosing to escape from Thoacdien and
live with fewer machines.

> We have come to the meadows as our first
> genuine rudeness. We have said no to all
> systems good or bad, and to all who run
> systems, good or bad. I came to the
> meadows when I . . . embraced the fact of
> my basic goodness, my basic and first
> desire to be positive -- which is possible
> -- in a universe where most other persons

Lyman Tower Sargent

> want the same. I had almost come to
> believe that I did need an artificial
> framework for my life . . . in order to
> survive (p. 298).

The real problem is with those -- human or
"computer" -- who control people either directly
through violence or power or more indirectly through
belief. The human art is to free oneself from
oppression whether that oppression is direct or
extremely subtle, as under Thoacdien.

Thea Plym Alexander

The emphasis on a higher state of consciousness is
also found in the only one of the eutopias under
consideration which has had a movement founded to bring
eutopia and reality together. Thea Plym Alexander's
2150 A. D. (1971)[18] has been ignored by scholars even
more than the rest of these works, but it is similar to
them since it stresses anarchism and equality between
the sexes. It is different both in the degree of
emphasis on the need to develop a higher consciousness
and in the movement. The author believes in her
eutopia; it is never entirely clear that the authors of
the other works believe in theirs.
The basis for *2150 A. D.* is a complex set of
religious, spiritual or metaphysical beliefs starting
from the basic premise "all is one" (p. 25).

> Macro philosophy is a system for
> relating all things from the smallest
> (micro) to the largest (macro). It begins
> something like this: All things are not
> only related but macrocosmically one.
> Things are only separate and divisible
> from micro viewpoints or frames of
> reference. Macro philosophy envisions a
> microcosmic-macrocosmic continuum (m-M
> continuum) in which neutrons, protons, and

----

[18]Thea Plym Alexander, *2150 A. D.* Tempe, Ariz.: Macro
Books, 1971.

electrons are indivisible parts of ever
larger physical bodies such as man.
Continuing, we can perceive man as an
indivisible part of a third planet called
Earth, and then (again enlarging our
perspective) we can perceive this planet
as an indivisible part of a solar system
which is, in turn, an indivisible part of
a galaxie which is an indivisible part of
a . . . and so on (p. 253).

The point of all this is that the human race is
cut off from wholeness, and, thus, feels anxiety, pain,
loneliness, etc., and a way must be found to bring
about the possibility of wholeness. For example, and
at a low level, wholeness is found in sexual
intercourse since the soul is androgynous or perfectly
balanced between male and female. For the soul's
periodic sojourns on this earth (reincarnation has been
proven), it divides into male and female. Therefore,
sexual intercourse is a low level (micro) means of
achieving wholeness. There are two other levels in
addition to the micro -- sub-macro and macro. The
whole purpose of society in 2150 is to enhance the
higher selves, particularly the Macro.

As a result, this society has a clearly defined
hierarchy dependent upon levels of awareness, but
within the framework of wholeness -- the Macro Family.
The complex structure that is the Macro Family is
designed to both illustrate the levels of awareness and
the potential progression of individuals as they reach
higher and higher levels of consciousness. This
process is the result of an educational system
beginning at birth and ending (as a formal system) at
age thirty.

Each three year period from birth through thirty
is treated as a separate learning period. The greatest
stress is laid on the early years with the first two
triads given the most attention.

As the child gets older, the help of those with
higher awareness continues with individual Macro
counseling. Other education is primarily through an
interactive computer followed by discussion with peers
and counselors. Later, vocational activities are
added, together with expanded periods of solitary
contemplation.

Macro Society is highly advanced technically -- so

that robots do all the dirty work. In addition, more advanced individuals are capable of psychokinesis. Therefore, they don't even have to physically push any buttons. They do that mentally.

All factories are run by servo mechanisms; there is no economic competition, this being one large family. Considerably fewer products are produced. There is no money and no private property. Thus, there is no waste and all effort can be directed at human improvement.

There is no government and no formal religion. There is obviously no need for police or military, law or lawyers, churches or bureaucracies.

All human races have been deliberately blended into one by choosing the best characteristics from each race. This also eliminates the possibility of racism.

Individuals live as couples from their earliest years. Sex tends to be promiscuous at first but becomes monogamous as individuals mature.

The spiritual emphasis of *2150 A. D.* is a bit unusual, but the life presented is not much different from the life found in the other works. The society of the future is not perfect. First, there are still some micro types around (isolated on an island). Second, the people of the highest awareness are only beginning to develop.

Marge Piercy[19]

The best written and in many ways the most interesting of these novels is Marge Piercy's *Woman on the Edge of Time* (1976).[20] Piercy's novel has a main

----

[19]On Piercy, see Rachel Blau DuPlessis, "The Feminist Apologues of Lessing, Piercy, and Russ," *Frontiers*, 4, No. 1 (Spring, 1979), pp. 1-8; Nadia Khouri, "The Dialectics of Power: Utopia in the Science Fiction of Le Guin, Jeury, and Piercy," *Science-Fiction Studies*, 7 (March 1980), pp. 49-60; Susan Kress, "In and Out of Time: The Form of Marge Piercy's Novels," in *Future Females*, pp. 109-122; and Pearson, "Beyond Governance."
[20]Marge Piercy, *Woman on the Edge of Time*. New York: Alfred A. Knopf, 1976; edition used -- New York:

character, Connie Ramos, a poor, Chicano patient in a
New York mental hospital. She "travels" to a future
world which is an anarchist eutopia. Connie's life has
been horrendous in the contemporary United States but
not much different than that of most poor Chicano
women.
     Woman on the Edge of Time is the most complete of
the eutopias, showing a fully functioning society and
most of its institutions. To Connie Ramos it seems
primitive.

> She saw . . . a river, little no account
> buildings, strange structures like long-
> legged birds with sails that turned in the
> wind, a few large terracotta and yellow
> buildings and one blue dome, irregular
> buildings, none bigger than a supermarket
> in her day, an ordinary supermarket in any
> shopping plaza. The bird objects were the
> tallest things around and they were
> scarcely higher than some of the pine
> trees she could see. A few lumpy free-
> form structures with green vines (p. 68).

     The "bird objects" are windmills and symbolize the
concern with what we call "alternative energy sources."
This point is made in most of these eutopias, but
Piercy makes it most strongly. First, the future has
as part of its past a few of our disasters, nuclear and
otherwise. The world is still recovering from our
farming methods and our pollution. Second, no one in
the future would ask another person to go down into
mines to get coal or metals. Human life and health are
more important than what the mines could provide and
substitutes will just have to be found or the resources
will be done without.
     Decisions of that sort are made socially. This is
an anarchist society; it cooperates among both its
individual members and communities. Localities make
their own decisions about their own areas. Individuals
are chosen by lot to serve on a local council for a

Fawcett. For a dystopia by Piercy see *Dance the Eagle to
Sleep*. New York: Fawcett/Crest, 1970. See also her
Vida and *Braided Lives* for related nonutopian works.

term of a year -- ". . . threemonth with the rep before
you and three with the person replacing you and six
alone" (p. 151). Each council includes an individual
designated to speak for the earth and another to speak
for animals. These individuals are chosen by lot from
among those who have dreamed they will fulfill this
role.

The council is not authoritarian. Decisions are
made only after there is agreement. "After a big
political fight, we guest each other. . . .The winners
have to feed the losers and give presents" (pp.
153-154). Questions involving wider geographic areas
(and they are careful to recognize the potential
effects of their decisions on others) are reached
through consultations with everyone who could be
involved. "How can people control their lives without
spending a lot of time in meetings" (p. 154).

Most of the questions Piercy mentions being
discussed refer to either economic-ecological problems
or, in the past, general questions regarding the number
and kind of children to be produced. In this society,
which is far advanced in biological technology,
children are not carried by women but are machine bred.
This way the society controls the genetic makeup of the
population and thus, for example, has been able to rid
itself of the possibility of racism.

As a result each child has three mothers (men are
mothers also) and are raised by the three until they go
through a rite of passage to independence. Due to the
biological advances, both men and women are able to
breastfeed children.

> It was part of women's long revolution.
> When we were breaking all the old
> hierarchies. Finally there was that one
> thing we had to give up too, the only
> power we ever had, in return for no more
> power for anyone. The original
> production: the power to give birth.
> 'Cause as long as we were biologically
> enchained, we'd never be equal. And males
> would never be humanized to be loving and
> tender. So we all became mothers. Every
> child has three. To break the nuclear
> bonding (p. 105).

Children are raised communally with a great deal

of involvement by the elderly, who the society feels are particularly able to understand children. Education is constant and involves learning the sorts of things necessary to live in a society close to nature and dependent on an understanding of nature to succeed. In our terms, the education sounds like vocational education, but it produces, as our version tends not to, sensitive, artistic fully human beings.

Every individual in the society gets a year off every seventh year to do pretty much as they wish. They are freed from productive labor in order to sit back and take stock or undertake some project they've been wanting to undertake when the time was available.

Within the context of a balanced ecology, the economy is highly automated. The people believe that the human being is dehumanized by factory life and choose to use some of their scarce energy resources to run some factories. As an alternative, they would prefer to do without.

In some ways, Piercy's future society seems limited, but on inspection the limits are freely chosen to keep people from having to do what they would not choose to do. Luxuries are limited. Some such luxuries circulate throughout the community from lending libraries; others are simply used less often. The society can choose to produce more of some luxury item if it wishes.

Piercy's society is the most fully realized of these societies, but it is not perfect. There are conflicts and jealousies; these are human beings with the full range of human emotion. They live in a healthy society and, as a result, are themselves healthy most of the time.

Joanna Russ[21]

----

[21]On Russ, see Douglas Barbour, "Joanna Russ's *The Female Man*: An Appreciation," *The Sphinx*, No. 13, vol. 4, (1981), pp. 67-75; Barbour, "Patterns of Meaning in the SF Novels of Ursula K. Le Guin, Joanna Russ and Samuel R. Delany, 1962-1972," Diss., Queen's University, Kingston, Ontario, Canada, 1976; DuPlessis, "The Feminist Apologues," and Natalie M. Rosinsky, "A Female Man? The 'Medusan' Humor of Joanna Russ,"

Lyman Tower Sargent

With *The Female Man* (1975),[22] we find a different
emphasis. *The Female Man* is a strong, clear, angry
statement of radical feminism stressing the damage done
to women by our social arrangements. It also provides
a picture of a good society, Whileaway, where there are
no men. There have been a number of works recently
presenting such societies.[23]
Most of these single sex societies are not
anarchist, but two come close, Russ's *The Female Man*
and Charnas's *Motherlines*. *The Female Man*, in
particular, shares the general attitudes expressed in
the rest of these works. This justifies its discussion
here, but there are also differences in emphasis.
The form of *The Female Man* presents four different
time lines. The four female characters are identical
genetically and the extreme differences they exhibit
are socially determined. They are Joanna from our
time, Jeannine from a world where there was no World
War II and the depression continues, Janet from
Whileaway, and Jael from a world where there is a
constant war (literally, not figuratively) between men
and women. For my purposes, the most interesting
person is Janet.
Whileaway is a free, equal and secure society.[24]
There are relatively few rules and regulations,
although there are some and those few are enforced.
Generally, what limits on behavior there are are

Extrapolation, 23, No. 1 (Spring 1982), pp. 31-36.
[22] Joanna Russ, *The Female Man*. New York: Bantam, 1975.
[23] See, for example, Suzy McKee Charnas's *Motherlines*
(1978), Sally Miller Gearhart's *The Wanderground*
(1978), Rochelle Singer's *The Demeter Flower* (1980); and
Donna J. Young's *Retreat* (1979).
[24] An earlier story "When It Changed," in *Again,
Dangerous Visions*, pp. 253-260, uses the same setting but
gives the planet a significantly different history.
Men return before Whileaway is ready. A later novel,
The Two of Them. New York: Berkley, 1978, shows
another society in which women are suppressed. This is
a sequel to Suzette Haden Elgin's "For the Sake of
Grace," *Magazine of Fantasy and Science Fiction*, 36, No. 5
(May 1969), pp. 77-97.

established mores rather than laws. A fairly elaborate code of behavior is implied but most breaches of this unwritten code are settled between individuals, through duels.

Children are born to women of about thirty. They are born into families of about thirty members. At age four or five, they are sent to regional schools for practical education. At puberty, they are turned loose -- most travel, explore, or go to live off the land. At seventeen, they join the labor force and are sent where they are most needed. At twenty-one, they can move to more complex jobs, begin apprenticeships, marry into an existing family or form their own. By twenty-five, she will have joined or formed a family and thereby chosen her geographic base. She will grow old traveling, loving, working. In old age she will shift to more sedentary jobs. The work week is about sixteen hours with rarely more than three hours on one job.

There are undescribed geographical and professional parliaments, but they obviously have little to do. The women of Whileaway take care of themselves.

Whileaway as a society has great respect for technology. The people have used technology to free themselves from the worst kinds of work and to give themselves more time for living. People mostly live on farms because farm work doesn't allow for the neat scheduling other work does. It is a good life.

In an earlier story, "Nobody's Home" (1972),[25] Russ describes a future world in which the key technological change is a transporter system which allows an individual to move instantaneously between any two places on earth. The society is without scarcity and has a tremendous amount of individual freedom. The story focuses on the development of an extended family system. The family is made up of individuals, both related and unrelated, who have been invited to join the group by any member of the group. Their continued existence within the family depends

----

[25]"Nobody's Home," in *New Dimensions II*, ed. Robert Silverberg (Garden City: Doubleday, 1972), pp. 1-20. Reprinted: *Women of Wonder: Science Fiction Stories by Women About Women*, ed. Pamela Sargent (New York: Vintage, 1974), pp. 235-256.

upon acceptance of the group as a whole. The family allows for considerable diversity in temperament and personality, but a high level of intelligence is essential. The family rarely spends time together, except when a new member is introduced, but it can be brought together at any time. The family is made up of every age group. They practice bisexual group sex within the family, and one of the practices on acceptance of a new member involves sexual relations with many members of the family.

Suzy McKee Charnas

Suzy McKee Charnas has written two books using roughly the same setting, *Walk to the End of the World* (1974) and *Motherlines* (1978).[26] The former is a dystopia in which a post-disaster society (called the Holdfast) suppresses women in a particularly vicious manner. *Motherlines* presents two societies of free women living outside the Holdfast, which is failing. Charnas's main concern in *Motherlines* is with a society of horsewomen who lead a mostly nomadic life. The other society is the "free-fems," women who have escaped from the Holdfast.

The nomadic society of *Motherlines* is not perfect. There are conflicts and jealousies, but they are contained by a net of customs which makes acceptable resolutions of conflicts possible. There are rules, but the rules are generally limited to what is necessary to survive in a hostile environment.

Each person lives embedded in a network of close relationships with other women who form families and provide the support each individual needs. Children are raised by all women in these families. As soon as possible, children leave the families to run freely with other children, but they do so within the physical protection of the entire society.

One of the emphases in these novels has been equality between women and men. Obviously this is not

----

[26]Suzy McKee Charnas, *Walk to the End of the World*. New York: Ballantine, 1974; and *Motherlines*. New York: Berkley, 1978.

the case in either *The Female Man* or *Motherlines*. Here
the emphasis is on what might be called the empowerment
of women. This contrasts sharply in stated intent from
Piercy's notion of taking power away from everyone, but
the results are not too different. In both approaches
individuals have more control of themselves and no one
has much of any power to coerce anyone else.

Conclusion

    I have looked at a number of recent anarchist
eutopias written by women and which can reasonably be
described as feminist.[27] There are other works by women
which could have been included, most notably Doris
Lessing's ongoing *Canopus in Argos: Archives* series,
which is not so much anarchist but apolitical, and a
number of works that depict societies without men which
are not at all anarchist.[28] There are also a number of
books by men that could be discussed here.[29] I have
chosen to limit my discussion to the particular works
here both to avoid an intolerable length and because
these are, I think, both the best and the most

----

[27]The only previous study which discusses these books
in similar terms is Carol Pearson, "Women's Fantasies
and Feminist Utopias," *Frontiers*, 2, No. 3 (1977), pp.
50-61. For various comments on women in science
fiction, see Susan Janice Anderson, "Feminism and
Science Fiction: Beyond BEMs and Boobs," in *Aurora;
Beyond Equality*, ed. Anderson and Vonda N. McIntyre
(Greenwich, Ct.: Fawcett, 1976), pp. 11-15; Pamela J.
Annas, "New Worlds, New Words: Androgyny in Feminist
Science Fiction" *Science-Fiction Studies*, 5 (July 1978),
pp. 143-156; Mary Kenny Badami, "A Feminist Critique of
Science Fiction," *Extrapolation*, 18,No. 1 (December
1976), pp. 6-19; Marleen Barr (ed.) *Future Females: A
Critical Anthology*. Bowling Green, O.: Bowling Green
State University Popular Press, 1981; Phyllis J. Day,
"Earthmother/Witchmother: Feminism and Ecology
Renewed," *Extrapolation*, 23,No. 1 (Spring 1982), pp.
12-21; Beverly Friend, "Virgin Territory: The Bonds and
Boundaries of Women in Science Fiction," in *Many
Futures Many Worlds: Theme and Form in Science Fiction*, ed.

representative of anarchist feminist eutopias.
    In conclusion, I want to point to the basic issues
these works raise and some of the solutions they
suggest to the problems identified. One of the
problems, to which many of the answers are negative, is
whether men and women can live in the same society on
the basis of equality. It may not be quite impossible,
but men in particuilar are going to have to change
dramatically if a healthy society is to be possible.
Remember Piercy's notion that men will have to change
biologically.
    Equality must be achieved for freedom to be
possible, and vice versa. All these works emphasize
that freedom and equality go together; they are not
separate or separable.
    All these works also stress that the human race
must get in tune with nature. Ecology will be the
constant concern of the future.
    Related to the ecological theme is what seems to
be an area of contradiction found in most of the
novels, what can be called technological agrarianism.[30]
Technology is used to help free humankind from drudgery
and return us to contact with nature. If not
necessarily contradictory, technological agrarianism at

Thomas D. Clareson ([Kent. O.:] Kent State University
Press, 1977), pp. 140-163; Anne Hudson Jones, "Women in
Science Fiction: An Annotated Secondary Bibliography,"
Extrapolation, 23, No. 1 (Spring 1982), pp. 83-90; Lee
Cullen Khanna, "Women's Worlds: New Directions in
Utopian Fiction," *Alternative Futures*, 4, No. 2-3
(Spring/Summer 1981), pp. 47-60; Patricia Monk,
"Frankenstein's Daughters: The Problems of the Feminine
Image in Science Fiction," *Mosaic*, 13, No. 3-4 (Spring-
Summer 1980), pp. 15-27; Ellen Morgan, "The Feminist
Novel of Androgynous Fantasy, *Frontiers*, 2, No. 3 (Fall
1977), pp. 40-49: Joanna Russ, "The Image of Women in
Science Fiction," in *Images of Women in Fiction*: *Feminist
Perspectives*, ed. Susan Koppelman Cornillon (Bowling
Green, O.: Bowling Green State University Popular
Press, 1972), pp. 79-94; Jessica Amanda Salmonson,
"Introduction: Our Amazon Heritage," in *Amazons*! ed.
Salmonson (New York: Daw, 1979), pp. 7-15; Pamela
Sargent, "Women in Science Fiction," *Futures*, 7
(October 1975), pp. 433-441; and, of course, the other

least suggests a tension, perhaps unrecognized, which pervades the utopias -- science and technology is supposed to save us from science and technology. The positive point being made is that science and technology used for human ends is not enslaving but freeing. When it uses us (the norm today), it is a danger. In these societies, that will not happen.

There is a possible explanation for the appearance of this seeming contradiction in feminist utopias. On the one hand, women are often represented as being closer to nature than men. This "closeness to nature" shows up in a number of places in these utopias. For example, while Marge Piercy wants both women and men closer to nature, she stresses the special role of women in healing. Also, a number of science fiction and fantasy novels, such as Vonda N. McIntyre's *Dreamsnake* (1978), stress the re-emergence of traditinal powers held by women. Witchcraft (the craft of the wise) and healing are the most common examples.

On the other hand, technological change and scientific invention have dramatically changed the pattern of women's lives. "Labor-saving devices" around the home do, in spite of all the jokes about them, save labor and, as a result, space has been opened up in the lives of many women. Perhaps even more important, improvements in contraceptive technology have provided women with much greater

----

essays in this volume.
[28]See, for example, Cecilia Holland, *Floating Worlds*, (1976), Marion Zimmer Bradley, *The Ruins of Isis (1978)*, Josephine Saxton, *The Travails of Jane Saint (1980)*, and the works listed above in note 23.
[29]See, for example, James Cooke Brown, *The Troika Incident* (1970), Alex Comfort, *Tetrach* (1980), and Bert Garskopf, *The Canbe Collective Builds a Be-Hive (1977)*.
[30]For this theme in American thought, see Leo Marx, *The Machine in the Garden: Technology and the Pastoral Ideal in America*. New York: Oxford University Press, 1964. On this theme in feminist utopias, see Krishan Kumar, "Primitivism in Feminist Utopias," *Alternative Futures*, 4, No. 2-3 (Spring/Summer 1981), pp. 61-66; and Howard P. Segal, "The Feminist Technological Utopia: Mary E. Bradley Lane's *Mizora* (1890)," *Alternative Futures*, 4, No. 2-3 (Spring/Summer 1981), pp. 67-72.

control over when or whether to have children. As a result, the tension suggested by technological agrarianism can perhaps best be seen as an attempt to synthesize at a new level two fundamental themes in feminist thought.

Another possibly unrecognized theme is population. In all these utopias the population is much lower than it is today. Are the writers implicitly recognizing a central problem? Can we achieve utopia only if most of us die off first? I certainly hope not, but that seems to be the implicit message.

Another common theme, this one clearly recognized, is a greater concern with spiritual questions than is usual in the history of utopian literature. What is presented is not religion in any formal sense; rather, it is a concern with transcendence, a rejection (contradicted by all the technology) of the material. Again, there may be an unresolved tension.

According to Carol Farley Kessler, this emphasis has been a constant theme in utopias written by women in the United States.[31] Rather like the concern with the traditional powers of women, or perhaps as part of the traditional powers of women, is a concern with something beyond the rational. In the utopias discussed here, this is best symbolized by dreaming. Dreaming puts us (but particularly women) in touch with some deeper level of being that helps overcome the flaws of reason. In the past this same point was made by the use of religion or spiritualism; today (probably as a result of psychoanalysis) dreaming is used.

A final issue is the fact that a number of these utopias question mothering, child-rearing and the traditional family.[32] Piercy argues that women had to

----

[31] See Carol Farley Kessler, "Introduction," in *Daring to Dream: Utopian Fiction by United States Women Before 1920*, ed. Kessler (London: Routledge and Kegan Paul, forthcoming Fall 1983).
[32] On the general theme of the family in political thought, see Jean Bethke Elshtain (ed.) *The Family in Political Thought*. Amherst, MA.: University of Massachusetts Press, 1982. On the specific point of the family in utopianism, see Sargent, "Utopia and the Family: A Note on the Family in Political Thought," in *Dissent and Affirmation: Essays in Honor of Mulford Q. Sibley*,

give up child bearing so that no one could have powers that others did not have. Mary Staton replaces the early stages of child rearing with technology. The point seems to be a desire to avoid dominance and dependence. If no one holds power over another as parent, but parenting takes place through an extended rather than a nuclear family, the child achieves an independent personality earlier than in our society and without the traumas of a severe psychological rite of passage. Still, a number of the writers (again Piercy is the best example) institutionalize a new rite of passage between childhood and adulthood. The point seems to be that rites are needed but ours are flawed.

Utopianism is a critical literature; it takes a stance against the present, and these novels are no exception. The central criticism is the suppression of women and the hypocrisy that surrounds all female-male relationships. All the other criticisms stem from this central one. We are used by our machines, we destroy our environment and ourselves, we pretend to be rational and are not and suppress the healthy emotion we might have. We preach freedom and equality and practice coercion, hierarchy and patriarchy. All in all, we are a mess. Life could be so much better.

----

ed. Arthur L. Kalleberg, J. Donald Moon, and Dan Sabia (Bowling Green, O.: Bowling Green State University Popular Press, forthcoming Summer 1983).

Most of the research on and writing of this essay was done while I was on a National Endowment for the Humanities grant at the Institute for Advanced Study, Princeton. I wish to thank the Endowment, the Institute and the University of Missouri-St. Louis for their support.

METHOD IN HER MADNESS:
FEMINISM IN THE CRAZY UTOPIAN
VISION OF TIPTREE'S COURIER

Carolyn Rhodes

In the "Introduction" to her study (*Madness and Sexual Politics in the Feminist Novel*, Madison: University of Wisconsin Press, 1978), Barbara Rigney features the feminist argument that "female insanity . . . can in a majority of cases be explained by the oppression of women in a power-structured, male supremacist society" (p. 6). Rigney quotes Kate Millet (from *Sexual Politics*) that "when in any group of persons, the ego is subjected to such invidious versions of itself through social beliefs, ideology, and tradition [as in the case of women] the effect is bound to be pernicious," and she cites also Phyllis Chesler's explanation that madness in women is "an intense experience of female biological, sexual, and cultural castration, and a doomed search for potency."

Thus, Rigney explains, "Freud's deterministic theories are denied, and the negative experience of women is seen [by modern feminists] as a cultural phenomenon rather than as an anatomical inevitability" (pp. 6-7). On the positive side, Rigney finds that R.D. Laing's "revolutionary approach to both philosophy and psychoanalysis can provide at least a terminology, a framework convenient for feminist protest" (p. 7). She then applies Laingian insights and theories to works by four women novelists: Bronte, Woolf, Lessing, and Atwood.

This paper treats the concept of madness that is dramatized in Raccoona Sheldon's short story "Your Faces, Oh My Sisters! Your Faces Filled of Light!," in *Aurora: Beyond Equality*, edited by Vonda N. McIntyre and Susan Janice Anderson (Greenwich, Conn.: Fawcett, 1977, pp. 16-35). Sheldon is actually Alice Sheldon, a retired experimental psychologist, whose work written under the pen-name James Tiptree, Jr., has been widely acclaimed. "Your Faces, Oh My Sisters!" blends utopian fantasies with stark depictions of repressive aspects of contemporary society. In this feminist story of a visionary journey undertaken by a woman who has, by conventional standards, actually gone mad, some of R. D. Laing's theories about madness are implicit. One of these is the idea that "the experience and behavior that gets labeled schizophrenic that is, madness is a special strategy that a person invents in order to live in an unliveable situation" (*The Politics of Experience*, New York: Ballantine, 1976, p. 115). Another is Laing's suggestion that "from the alienated starting point of our world's pseudo-sanity, everything is equivocal . . . . Let no one suppose," he asserts, "that we meet 'true' madness any more than we are truly sane" (p. 144). And finally, the transcendent aspects of the ending of Sheldon's story are consistent with Laing's observation that "madness need not be a breakdown. It may also be a breakthrough. It is potentially liberation and renewal as well as enslavement and existential death" (p. 133).

Sheldon's tightly constructed story moves through fifteen episodes, all presented omnisciently, but in two alternating patterns: a set limited to the perceptions of the mad, yet also visionary woman, throughout one long night, until dawn, and an alternating set, dramatizing others' observations and opinions about her behavior.

The episodes are short, particularly for the observers and those to whom they report, so that the story's pace is rapid. Although the passages that reveal the woman's mind are typically longer and quite different in tone, even the longest of these is just three pages, and the entire story is only twenty pages.

The eight episodes devoted to the meditations and preoccupations of the protagonist depict her joy as she strides westward across Chicago during a stormy night. Gradually, much aided by the comments of observers in the alternating episodes, readers realize that this "courier," as she perceives herself, is not moving through a glorious future, many years after the dissolution of the huge and threatening city, but is actually there in the 1970's, and in danger. She madly revises all of the turmoil and hostility surrounding her, as if it were peace and safety. The seven onlookers' segments alternate with these fantasies of

the courier, and include as well some subsequent
reports to the woman's physician and family and a
newspaperman. The author uses these normal observers
to make it piercingly clear that the blithe and
confident "courier" is mad. The woman's joy and trust
and self-assurance are her insanity. Also,
significantly, her claims to freedom and self-control
are likely to be judged as wicked and provocative.
Observers who know or suspect her of delusions make
kinder interpretations, but even among them, reproaches
are likely to accompany compassion. The free woman,
the woman at large in the open air, may be enjoying
herself, but to others she is mad, sad, or bad.

In her delusive world, the self-styled courier
imagines that she lives in a future idyllic period, a
time when people share the land and its simple
wholesome goods. In ways reminiscent of a romantic
view of the American Indians as noble savages, she
perceives an ecologically rich landscape around her.
Lines from Longfellow's "Hiawatha" stream through her
thoughts: she mulls over the delights of simple skills
and elemental values such as love for wise elders and
kinship between people and creatures of the wild.
Sheldon creates at first amusing and later terrifying
ironies in the courier's misperceptions: the middle-
aged woman who gives her a ride hardly appreciates
being called, however lovingly, "wrinkled old Nokomis";
and the courier is vulnerable to a gang of rapists
partly because she thinks they are just a pack of wild
dogs and presumes that they are well-fed enough not to
attack humans.

Every aspect of nature enchants the courier, and
she translates the urban blight into picturesque ruins.
Savoring the joys of woman in the open air, on the
move, she is transcendentally Whitmanesque, delighting
equally in rough weather and in the serene moonlight
that follows the storm. Her thoughts sparkle with
images of light as representative of beauty, wisdom,
and comfort: lightening, moonglow, and the break of
dawn all link her hopes with her basic faith that she
is surrounded by loving sisters. She serves them by
carrying mail and messages through the countryside and
the ruined cities; they love and appreciate her. Thus
everyone she meets is hailed as "Sister," whether male
or female, and all are seen as benevolent, fascinating
people.

In Sheldon's alternating sections, the sane react

to the courier (Laing would of course label them
"pseudo-sane"). These sections both highlight the
poignancy of her delusions and dramatize the starkness
of contemporary life, particularly for women who want
freedom.

Strangers see the courier as pitiful at best, and,
at worst, so wicked that she ought to be punished. For
example, according to the police who appear in two
episodes, merely her being outdoors alone at night
means that she deserves disaster. Other passers-by
feel mixtures of compassion and bafflement as they
realize how trusting she is toward everyone she meets,
and how self-confident she is in her journeying. One
man, a physician, recognizes the symptoms of her
"delusive systems," and correctly guesses that she has
undergone electro-shock therapy. The older woman who
thought her a hitchhiker and gave her a lift, later
regrets that kindness, suspects her of drug-taking, and
hopes she meets some dire fate. Two more empathic
women wish they could have helped her: the physician's
wife, and a prostitute. When the wife tells her
husband that the courier seemed "happy and free . . .
she was fun," the physician can only reply: "that's the
sick part, honey."

Yet from the author's sympathetic viewpoint, the
sickest parts are probably evident in the attitudes of
two women who might have helped by sharing the
courier's anguish or responding to her danger -- her
mother and a policewoman near the scene of the gang-
rape in which the courier is killed. The mother's
exasperation is heard before the daughter's fate is
certain. Although this parental anger is followed by
grief, the nature of the mother's complaints doubtless
summarize her attitudes throughout the progress of her
daughter's mental illness. She speaks in the voice of
a safe, well-provided-for, middle class woman, bitter
towards any female who wants to escape the shelter of
domesticity:

> What did she want? Always running away.
> Freedom. Doesn't she know you can't have
> freedom? Why isn't this world good enough
> for her? She had everything. If I can
> take it why can't she? (p. 29).

The mother's anger, of course, involves an
inconsistency: the claim that the world was "good

Carolyn Rhodes

enough," that the daughter "had everything," juxtaposed
with the sense of something endured by the mother that
the daughter couldn't take, but should have.
 The mother's judgements are poignant, but the
policewoman's decisions are despicable. Sheldon shows
the officer's failure to prevent violence and stresses
its horror as a decision taken by one woman refusing to
recognize the plight of another woman. The reporter
who later investigates the inaction of the police
officers who saw the gang following the courier seems
dumbfounded at the policewoman's attitudes. The female
officer refers to the rapists as "alleged assailants,"
speaks of the victim as "some little tramp," and
explains with irritation that she and her partner in
the police car could not leave their post of
surveillance to check on "pedestrians." Her angry
dismissal of the reporter reveals the premises
underlying her indifference to the fate of the victim:

>I'm not a nursemaid . . . don't care if
>she was crazy. A spoiled brat if you ask
>me, all those women's lib freaks. I work.
>Who does she think she is, running on the
>street at night? She thinks the police
>have nothing more important to do than
>that? (p. 32).

 The policewoman's disdain and emotional distance
repeats a theme established near the beginning of the
story. The character seen by the courier as "Old
Nokomis" went home to tell her daughter about the
unusual hitchhiker, commenting with disgust about her
casual ways: she must be "one of those bra-burners."
The two women, both wholly preoccupied with housewares
and cosmetics, chatter about "any girl like that" and
quite agree that breaking the rules of discreet
feminine behavior means that she is "just asking for
whatever she gets;" she deserves "no sympathy at all"
(p. 20).
 By the story's end, Sheldon has dramatized the
likelihood that when the public and the police and the
punks all see a free woman as "asking for" abuse, she
will get it. On the other hand, the author has enabled
readers to share in full the delusively happy
interpretations that the courier applies to the
cityscapes she sees. Also, readers are permitted to
share the courier's struggles not to see the

actualities that surround her: whenever she begins to
lapse into accurate perceptions of the threatening
world about her, the courier persuades herself that
these are hallucinations, "fever-nightmares" from the
past:

> Dreaming she was stuck back in history
> like a caged-up animal. An 'affluent young
> suburban matron,' whatever that was. All
> those weird people, telling her. Don't go
> outside, don't do this, don't do that,
> don't open the door, don't breathe.
> Danger everywhere (p. 29).
>   How did they *live* . . . . Those poor
> old sisters, never being free, never even
> being able to go walking! Well, those
> dreams really made history live and
> breathe for her . . . (p. 29).

The courier's madly-visionary perspective alters each
person and setting to fit her scenario of a joyous,
benevolent future. She perceives the prostitute she
meets as an historian of "the old days ... when people
had to sell their sex organs" to survive (p. 30). She
perceives current slums as long-empty relics of the
crowded crazy times (p. 31). And just as she revises
some of her own memories and observations to nightmares
sent forward through time to her, she also tries to
send back blessings to the tortured past, "back to the
poor maddened people who once strove here," feeling
that her happiness has come "somehow out of their
anguish" (p. 31).

By the time the story reaches its final ghastly
episode, Sheldon has also established a clear framework
of feminist values and suggested a utopian vision of
the future through the courier's madness, underlining
these values and the wholesomeness of the utopian
vision by the lack of sympathy that is shown by
negative characters in the story. The feminist values
and utopian vision blend with the ecological and
psychological as the woman moves through a world where
all people are kind and movement is unhampered and
danger no longer exists. Poverty, oppression and crime
no longer exist. The problems of patriarchal privilege
or masculine brutality no longer exist, since all
people are women, and are indeed sisterly women --
sharing and supportive. Men have all died out.

-39-

But it should not be inferred that the story is
anti-male or that the courier's madness results from
having been mistreated by any particular men. Her
husband and father are shown as decent people, more
sympathetic, for instance, than her woman physician, or
her mother, or the policewoman. It may be inferred,
however, that the feminist elements in "Your Faces, Oh
My Sisters!," that the courier's madness results from
pervasive oppression, the oppression defined by Rigney
as intrinsic to the "power-structured, male-supremacist
society" (p. 6).
    As the story unfolds, it becomes clear that the
courier's madness can be explained in Laingian terms as
"a special strategy that a person invents in order to
live in an unliveable situation" (p. 115). Sheldon,
however, provides few concrete details as to what made
the protagonist's life unliveable. Her past is
suggested by the outburst in which the courier's mother
asks: "Why isn't this world good enough for her? She
had everything. If I can take it why can't she?"
Another detail is added when the courier's father
attempts to calm his distraught wife: "She was out of
her head . . . . She wouldn't even recognize her own
baby" (p. 29). And there are suggestive hints in the
courier's "fever nightmares," her "dreaming she was
stuck back in history like a caged-up animal. An
'affluent young suburban matron,' whatever that was"
(p. 29).
    Sheldon makes no attempt to connect the courier's
blankness toward motherhood with her own mother's role
as would-be shaper of her daughter's personality toward
acceptance of things-as-they-are. But probably three
factors, first being an undutiful daughter, second an
unacknowledged mother, and third an autonomous woman
denying the world's restraints, can be linked in the
pattern of her madness, which is her freedom; the
courier escapes through psychotic fantasy to a world of
simple healthy out-door life. Somewhat like a female
Huck Finn, she will not be civilized. In her case,
civilization means urban and suburban life, and perhaps
the duty to shape her offspring to accept the
discontents of civilization and to hide from its
dangers.
    As has been noted, Sheldon does suggest the
painful role of the courier's mother toward her in a
psychological shaping, but mentions the courier's child
only as a precipitating cause for psychosis. Her

refusal to see contemporary life in its threatening guises is the courier's pervasive syndrome -- what Laing would call her "special strategy" invented "in order to live in an unliveable situation" (p. 115).

As Laing asserts in *Politics of Experience*: "Let no one suppose that we meet 'true' madness any more than we are truly sane" (p. 144). Given a feminist perspective, the validity of Laing's assertion is painfully evident throughout Sheldon's story. The madness of the courier is deliberately contrasted with the madness of contemporary life. Anyone who insists on living by elemental freedoms and wholeness of kinships, who insists on perceiving the human interwoven with animal and planetary wholeness, is bound to be hopelessly out of touch with things as they are. Such a person is shown to live in a society where trust of others is madness. Sisterly love, the love that inspires and pervades the courier's fantasy, fulfills the failed promise of brotherly love.

Granting that the courier is mad by sane measures, the story compels readers to ask a piercing question -- who is really crazier, someone who envisions a world of joy and safety and sharing, or all of those others who have accepted the restraints and brutalities, and insist on the duty of the visionary to adjust to the destructive, or be destroyed?

"Your Faces, Oh My Sisters! Your Faces Filled of Light!" ends with a terrifying death scene: the courier is raped and killed by a brutal gang, perceived by her as a pack of wild dogs. To some degree, her agony is relieved by the continuation of her visions of sisterhood. The transcendental aspects of the ending of "Your Faces, Oh My Sisters!" are consistent with Laing's observation that "madness need not be a breakdown. It may be a breakthrough. It is potentially liberation and renewal as well as enslavement and existential death" (p. 133). As the courier is pinned down by the rapists, she realizes that she is being murdered, yet she still clings to hope and visionary truth:

> . . . she sees . . . in the light, in the
> patches of sky . . . the beautiful faces
> of her sisters speeding to save her, to
> avenge her . . . she knows it is all
> right, it will all be fixed . . . this is
> just an accident -- and soon she, or

-41-

> someone like her, will be going on again .
> . . over the wide free Earth, courier to
> Des Moines and points west -- (p. 35).

Are these hopes of the courier, her certainties, simply further depictions of crazed optimism, or does Sheldon implicitly affirm the strength of sisterhood, and prophecy greater future strength?

Does an ironic and bitter tone underly the visionary relief at the story's terrible climax? After all, many who were seen as sisters earlier in the story were actually helpless or even cruel, distanced from the free woman by bafflement or ill-will. In addition, the author has elsewhere commented wryly on the tendency of feminists to overestimate the power of sisterhood: in a serious letter to *Frontiers*, a leading feminist journal, she said, "In most societies, and for most of history, sisterhood is about as powerful as wet Kleenex. It is only the power to exchange agonized glances" (2, No. 3, Fall 1977, p. 68).

My reading is that Sheldon does present the story sincerely as a consciousness-raising effort, both through the courier's dismal fate and through the theme of madness. Her madness is the madness of hope. Her death, rich with hope beyond pain, conveys two sides of the truth about women who sanely break rules and act independently. Indeed, they do risk ghastly retributions but they simultaneously foreshadow and embody a future when women will share the freedoms of a "wide free Earth," because women and men will develop powers to love without exploiting each other or the planet.

UTOPIA AT THE END OF A MALE CHAUVINIST DYSTOPIAN WORLD:
SUZY McKEE CHARNAS'S FEMINIST SCIENCE FICTION

Marleen Barr

A Brief Biocritical Introduction to Charnas

Suzy Mckee Charnas's science fiction does not include the genre's expected emphasis upon zap guns, warp drives, and bug-eyed blobs who devour partially undressed, distressed damsels. She creates female protagonists who are strong and mature -- and fully clothed -- women who have nothing to do with assorted pieces of imaginative hardware. One fact about Charnas accounts for her deviation from science fiction's standard characteristics: she is a feminist, an important contributor to feminist utopian (and dystopian) science fiction.

Both Charnas and science fiction's new feminist wave have generated controversy:

> Suzy McKee Charnas came to the attention of science fiction in a big way in 1974, when her first novel, *Walk to the End of the World* was published by Ballantine.
> A powerful book by any standards, *Walk* featured some fine prose, several superb characterizations, and one of the best realized and most brutishly unpleasant future societies in the history of the genre. The novel drew plaudits ... from some of science fiction's leading authors, and made the readers sit up and take notice in droves. It drew a lot of attention . . . to its hitherto unknown author, and marked her as a writer to watch.

Marleen Barr

> It also identified her with the most
> prominent and controversial literary
> movement of Seventies SF: feminism. . . .
> Feminism and feminist writing are the new
> wave of the Seventies. Equally dominant,
> sometimes equally controversial, and as
> certain to restructure the genre as the
> New Wave of the Sixties. . . . It turned
> out that *Walk* was only the first book of a
> trilogy that Charnas was writing. The
> second book, *Motherlines*, was even stronger
> . . . .[1]

All of Charnas's fiction is aptly characterized by
Harlan Ellison's term, "dangerous visions."
    However, her novels' depictions of permissive
sexuality do not appear to be the work of a woman who
is content with her patriarchally sanctioned marriage.
Yet she is. Suzy McKee Charnas is not a radical
feminist separatist. In fact, as she explains, her
life is far from radical:

> Clearly those readers who get upset by
> what I've been saying will consider me a
> radical of the more or less flame-shooting
> variety depending on how widely their
> attitudes and my own diverge. But . . . I
> wouldn't dream of claiming to be a radical
> now. In fact, where it counts, I lead
> almost exactly the life my mother (child
> of immigrants) wished for her kids: I'm
> married to a lawyer, inhabit a neat little
> adobe house in a great part of the
> country, travel a bit, write books, teach
> school, keep cats, cook pretty well, know
> some sharp and creative folks, am close to
> my two sisters and my step-kids, and sleep
> well nights. Aside from certain minor
> variations and a taste for being something
> of a social hermit, I'm a sample
> bourgeoise.
>   Even in my head I'm not a

----

[1]George R. R. Martin, *New Voices III* (New York: Berkley,
1980), pp. 79-80.

revolutionary. I like my comforts and my freedoms too well to risk them on the possibility of something far worse.[2]

She is the wife of a Harvard educated lawyer and the stepmother of two children. Her lifestyle is traditional; her fiction is quite contrary to tradition. This might explain why her radical "dangerous visions" also include a moderate viewpoint. For example, as I will explain in the following pages, *Walk*, whose protagonist, Alldera, is victimized by an exaggeratedly sexist dystopian social system, also includes a portrayal of men who suffer at the hands of other men. And, *Motherlines* is a feminist utopia whose female citizens are just as flawed as ordinary, nonutopian females.

Charnas's work reflects her experiences. She was born, raised, and educated in Manhattan. After completing her B.A. at Barnard College, she spent two years as a Peace Corps volunteer in Nigeria before completing an M.A. in teaching at New York University. She taught in Manhattan and did curriculum development for a drug treatment unit at Flower Fifth Avenue Hospital. After her marriage and move to New Mexico, she began to write in earnest. New York, New Mexico, and Nigeria appear as the settings of her fiction.

Although the Holdfast in *Walk to the End of the World* does not correspond to any real location, as Charnas explains in "A Woman Appeared," the novel is drawn from parts of real people: "So I had to make Alldera up, and I composed her using aspects of a friend from my school days and aspects of myself." She goes on to state that characters in *Motherlines* are also drawn from reality: ". . . each of the women in it first came, I think, not from literature but from life. They were not impressions from some other book changed for use in my own. Each began as a scrap of the appearance or behavior of a real woman in the real world."[3]

----

[2]Neal Wilgus, "*Algol* Interview: Suzy McKee Charnas," *Algol* (Winter 1978-79), 25.
[3]Suzy McKee Charnas, "A Woman Appeared," in *Future Females: A Critical Anthology*, ed. Marleen S. Barr (Bowling Green: Popular Press, 1981), pp. 104, 106. Further references will be followed by AWA and page number.

Marleen Barr

Aspects of people, aspects of the real world, are
logically quite important to a person such as Charnas
who is interested in teaching, the development of human
resources. Such human development also coincides with
her fiction. Charnas's work teaches people about
feminism and hence improves the quality of women's
lives. She, in turn, was influenced by the writing of
other women: "During that same winter of 1972-73 I was
doing what so many other women were doing and was
doing: reading books like Shulamith Firestone's *The
Dialectic of Sex* . . . and *Sisterhood is Powerful* by Robin
Morgan . . . and participating in consciousness
raising sessions with other women. As my own awareness
matured -- and my anger at finding myself trapped in
the powerless class of women -- Alldera pushed her way
more and more to the heart of the story I was writing,
changing everything around her as my own perspective on
her fictional world changed" (AWA. p. 104). Like
Firestone and Morgan, Charnas also raises
consciousnesses. Alldera is a catalyst for change.
Readers who meet her in *Walk* and *Motherlines* derive
insights about a woman's role, insights which inspire
self-improvement.
In fact, for general readers, *Walk* shares the
didactic function of Marilyn French's *The Women's Room*,
a novel which enlightened those women who did not have
direct access to feminist voices. Both Charnas and
French are professional educators whose fiction can
teach those who have much to learn about feminism.
The resemblance between Charnas's writing and
mainstream feminist fiction is more obvious than its
connection to most of the science fiction written by
men. When comparing Charnas's work to the
aforementioned French, for example, it is clear that
the dehumanized "fems" in *Walk* are extreme versions of
the women in *The Women's Room*. In addition, both
Motherlines and French's second novel, *The Bleeding Heart*,
discuss the advantages of a society dominated by
females. Dolores, the protagonist of *The Bleeding
Heart*, is, in some ways, a true-to-life version of the
strong and independent Riding Women in *Motherlines*. The
point is, then, that the most crucial fact about
Charnas's work is its feminist orientation, not the
fact that it is categorized as science fiction.
And, oddly enough, like mainstream feminist
writing, alien life forms do not appear in Charnas's
science fiction. As all of Charnas's professional

activities point to her interest in human development, her fiction analyzes the meaning of the word "human": it presents an intermingling of the dichotomy separating man from beast. Men in *Walk* act like beasts while the women are treated like animals whose place in society is lower than that of southern plantation slaves. The juxtaposition of "man" with "beast" is even more pervasive in *Motherlines* where stallion semen creates female life. My following discussion of these novels, Charnas's utopian and dystopian feminist science fiction visions, illustrates her concern with the veneer of civilization. I will explain how these works speak out against the idea that women are somehow inferior to men.

Walk and *Motherlines* have enlightened their author about this pervasive culture misconception. No longer can Charnas accept her "culture's definition of women as a very limited type of people doing very limited things" (AWA. p. 105):

> As a result of writing *Walk* and *Motherlines* I think I have changed my way of looking at real women in the real world. When I meet a woman for the first time now, I am less likely than formerly to see only the feminine role that our culture allows her and more likely to glimpse her individuality and potentiality.
>
> Another result is a change in the way I make judgments about women writers -- myself included -- and their work. We do not, I think, just shrug off the conditioning of the patriarchal society at will. Most of us have our demons to exorcise -- dusty, internalized patterns of masculinist thinking and creating. Beyond the demons lies the green prospect of writing fiction about women as they really are and women as they might become (AWA. p. 107-108).

Charnas successfully writes such fiction.

As Charnas herself has been changed by writing, her readers also have the potential to make changes in their own lives. In this way, the recognition of the new feminist science fiction authors, the analysis of the new feminist utopias they envision, can facilitate

Marleen Barr

the creation of a new nonsexist dominant culture.
Robert Scholes's conclusion to *Fabulation and Metafiction*
explains that science fiction challenges literary -- as
well as cultural -- forms:

> From the field of science fiction, in
> particular, new writers have been emerging
> to join the ranks of literary fabulators,
> bringing both a concern for the
> traditional values of story-telling and a
> fresh vision of human problems and
> aspirations. From this point on, anyone
> interested in studying fabulative
> literature will have to consider writers
> like Ursula Le Guin, John Brunner, Philip
> K. Dick, Kate Wilhelm and a host of others
> who have matured and flourished all around
> us while our attention was focused on more
> 'reputable' authors. It has always been
> this way. From its beginning prose
> fiction has emerged from the despised
> world of popular culture to challenge the
> established literary forms. The modern
> novel itself arose in this way. That the
> process still continues is in itself a
> most heartening sign.[4]

Charnas deserves to have a prominent place on Scholes's
list: her work, which shocked many science fiction
editors, challenges the literary forms of the science
fiction -- as well as the patriarchal biases of
contemporary American society.

Walk to the End of the World

   Walk to the End of the World presents a nightmare of
contrasting extremes in a post-holocaust dystopian
society where women are enslaved by men. The nonwhite
"evil races"-- and even the animals -- cease to exist
after "the Wasting of the World." In the "Holdfast,"

----

[4]Robert Scholes, *Fabulation and Metafiction* (Urbana:
University of Illinois Press, 1979), p. 222.

Charnas's Feminist Science Fiction

the last remnant of civilization, white women
experience the deprivation which was once reserved for
people of color. Their situation is analogous to an
exaggerated version of contemporary sexism. Holdfast
women have replaced the underclass; men have replaced
the animals. All inhabitants of the Holdfast suffer.
    The Holdfast's masculine cultural hegemony is
quite frightening because Charnas's criticism of our
own society is easy to recognize. Her voice is
analogous to that of Stanislaw Lem in *The Star Diaries.*
Both authors stress the same point: man -- not some
outlandish alien -- is the true Bug-Eyed Monster. Here
is how Homo sapiens are described in Lem's novel: " .
. . he [a nonhuman delegate to The United Planets] told
of the massacres, pogroms, wars, crusades, genocides .
. . technologies of crime, instruments of torture . .
. . When he started in on the present day, sixteen
assistants had to wheel in carts that groaned beneath
stacks of additional documentation; . . . I [a
representative from Earth] began . . . to fear my very
self, as if, thrown in among these phantasmagorical,
outlandish beings that surrounded me on every side, *I*
were the only monster.'"[5] The delegate's accusations
are, of course, all true. *Walk* also enumerates truths
of human civilization: slavery, exploitation, burning
of women, rape, drug dependence, institutional stifling
of creativity, sexual perversion, pogroms, Nazi-like
research on human subjects, and nuclear devastation.
It is not a happy book. Charnas's vision of the
relationship between men and women mirrors the
grotesque.
    Oddly enough, although *Walk* is a feminist novel,
Alldera is not introduced until page sixty-six. And,
the section which is written from her point of view
appears close to the text's conclusion. Eykar Bek's
search for his father at first seems to form the
narrative's main focus. Two men accompany him on his
journey: Servan d Layo the darkdreamer, and Kelmz,
captain of the animalistic police force called
"Rovers." Alldera serves the three men. Before she
speaks, before readers meet her, these men have already
epitomized the horrors of their dystopian patriarchal

----

[5]Stanislaw Lem, *The Star Diaries* (New York: Avon, 1975),
p. 36.

society. But, despite this nonfeminist narrative
structure, once Alldera does speak, she assumes her
place at the novel's center. The male characters
become indistinguishable, fused and devoid of strong
individual characteristics; readers of *Walk* remember
Alldera.

And they remember her suffering at the hands of
men. However, Alldera and her fellow fems are not the
only victims in the Holdfast. Young men are also
exploited. Powerful older men strive to keep their
juniors powerless: "Everything the [male governing]
Board does -- or fails to do -- is calculated to insure
that nothing happens to shake its control. That means
no new ideas and no new territories and not too many
young men. . . . What's hierarchy for, if not to
dissipate young men's energy? Which is kept low anyhow
with insufficient diet, since the old men take more of
their share of the pittance of food that the Holdfast
furnishes."[6] Thus, *Walk* does not simply stop short at
labeling men as the enemy. It is a very broad-minded
feminist novel which takes care to illustrate that
women are not the only victims of patriarchal
repression.

Nor does it assume that all women are "sisters,"
that all women will support each other merely because
they are women. The plain-looking, highly intelligent
Alldera shares little in common with the beautiful "pet
fems" and the ignorant "working fems" who accompany her
on the journey to locate Bek's father. Alldera's
individuality, not a desire to conform to the behavior
of other women, is stressed. She escapes from the
Holdfast because of abilities which transcend gender:
mental acumen and physical endurance. Alldera is an
androgynous individual who survives because she has
developed her mind and her body to their fullest
capacity.

Since she accomplished this self-improvement in
the repressive Holdfast, her achievement is not to be
taken lightly. Although Alldera was trained to be a
runner, she has difficulty training her mind in a
society where women are systematically prevented from

----

[6] Suzy McKee Charnas, *Walk to the End of the World* (New
York: Ballantine, 1974), p. 190). Further references
will be followed by W and page number.

learning and from directly expressing their thoughts. Like blacks in the Jim Crow south, fems are crippled by the imposition of a language which is indirect and submissive: ". . .the majority of them [fems] were held to be incapable of any but the most limited fem-to-master type of speech. . . . 'This fem feels that they are all in the men's compound, please-you-master,' she [a fem] whined, slurring her words in the manner of fems'" (W. p. 53). Their speech is an exaggerated version of what Robin Lakoff defines as "women's language." The language used by fems illustrates Lakoff's notion that "looking at the way we customarily talk . . . about women whoever we are, we can gain insight into the way we feel . . . about women -- through close analysis of what we say and how we say it . . . ."[7]

Thus, it is logical to assume that Holdfasters would routinely use words like "cunt hunger" and "fem taint." Here is the novel's first reference to a woman: "Go eat fem shit" (W. p. 10). These derogatory utterances conform to our linguistic reality: women have "been known by beasts' names: Bird, Cat, Chick, Sow, Filly, Tigress, Bitch, Cow. . ." (W. p. 112). Real women are figuratively silenced; some fems are literally silenced: their tongues are cut out. "Muteness in fems was a fashion in demand among masters" (W. p. 141).

Despite the fact that men silence them, the fems have managed to create their own feminine subculture. Fems sing about their lives in the manner of black spirituals and workers' strike songs. But their words are muffled: "Every song needed one fem in the group who knew the words, and could sing them under the camouflage of gutterals and trills set up by the others to mask the sense of the song from men. . ." (W. p. 157). Their garbled words form a marked contrast to the proud "self-songs" sung by the Riding Women in *Motherlines.*

Even though the fems' songs function as a mutual support system, the following question is not easily answered: "How valuable could one fem be to other

----

[7]Robin Lakoff, *Langauge and Woman's Place* (New York: Harper and Row, 1975), p. 1. Further references will be followed by L and page number.

Marleen Barr

fems?" (W. p. 68). Since, in an environment where food
is scarce, they have learned to derive nutrition from
breast milk, there is some interdependence between
fems. And, some fems do try to band together to
subvert men's power. But, one the whole, an
animalistic fight for survival, rather than
cooperation, characterizes the fems' behavior toward
one another. More directly stated, those young fems
who fail to scrounge for their food on the straw-
covered "kit pit" floor will not survive. The most
independent and strong willed young fems also will not
survive. They are killed by older fems who fear the
future consequences of the youngsters' potential to
rebel. However, as opposed to the senior men who
fulfill their sexual desire with castrated boys (W. p.
79), no fem ever exploits another solely for self-
satisfaction.

Alldera is lucky. She has survived the kit pits;
she does not have to survive the "rendery" where women
are milked as if they were docile cows. Like the women
who are imprisoned and forced to produce children in
Kate Wilhelm's *Where Late the Sweet Birds Sang*, for
rendery fems, biology absolutely becomes destiny.
Alldera is thankful not to find herself in such a
situation. Alldera the runner will not be hindered by
her body.

This physical ability enables her to escape from
the Holdfast. Before she starts her run into the
unknown, she thinks about d Layo fleeing from 'Troi, a
ravaged Holdfast city: "So strong was her impression of
a hunting predator that she pictured d Layo cutting
down some less clever survivor and feeding on the
flesh, rank or not: and so he would, if necessary, as
innocently ruthless as any beast . . . there was
something primeval in the thought of the survivors
stalking one another among the ruins -- all hunters,
all quarry" (W. p. 213). But, ironically, 'Troi -- and
the entire Holdfast -- was a ruin even before society
crumbles in the novel's final pages. All Holdfast
citizens are survivors who feed upon other survivors,
all hunters, all quarry. The world's "Dirties, the
unmen," did not perish after the "Wasting." The
Holdfasters are all beast who stalk each other among
the ruins of civilization. In contrast, when Alldera
runs into an unknown new world, no one pursues her, and
she, in turn, pursues no one.

Charnas's Feminist Science Fiction

* * *

It is necessary to explain the presence of the
novel's violence and brutality. Charnas comments upon
contemporary society by exaggerating the truth, a
technique used by Jonathan Swift in "A Modest
Proposal." Both authors' texts refer to women as if
they were domestic animals. *Walk*: "Now, what do you
think would have happened if the bitch had dropped a
fem-cub?" (W. p. 40). "A Modest Proposal": " . . . a
child just dropped from its dam may be supported by her
milk for a solar year." And both texts shock readers
when they suggest appropriate food sources. Swift, of
course, proposes that society would benefit if babies
were eaten; Bek's father proposes to feed upon the
flesh of women. He is serious:

> 'Flavor, flavor. . . . Haven't you been
> listening? I'm talking economy, total
> utilization of the few resources that are
> going to be left to us. You can't run a
> Reconquest on bulk-food like grain, so you
> use throw-back fems as meat, a food that
> young men can pack in quantity on long
> expeditions. We're going to rationalize
> society into small groups of superior men
> subsisting primarily on the meat, skins
> and muscle power of a mass of down-bred
> fems' (W. p. 203).

His suggestion: fems are to be systematically
exterminated. Women, the Holdfast's final solution.

I am now drawn back to my introduction's
comparison of Charnas with Marilyn French. French's
Dolores also equates sexisim with Nazism:

> But women must keep their bad feelings
> about men locked up, the outside world is
> hostile to them. . . . To be a woman in
> such a world is to be an occupied
> population with the Nazis in control
> everywhere. . . . 'Are you saying all men
> are Nazis by birth? . . . are you saying
> all men are Nazis' and she [Dolores] . . .
> she would have to say *yes*"[8]

Marleen Barr

Her extreme point of view brings Charnas's following
comment to mind: *Walk* "ended up being about sexism
carried to a logical extreme, and it suggests, I hope,
the inherent destructiveness of any society in which
one portion of the population enslaves and dehumanizes
another" (AWA. p. 104). The novel does successfully
suggest the inherent destructiveness of sexism. And,
in terms of Swift, we can understand that the extreme
dehumanization of women depicted in *Walk* can indeed
become an actuality. The following exaggerated
conception in "A Modest Proposal" became a truth of our
century: "Those who are more thrifty. . . may flay the
carcass; the skin of which artificially dressed will
make admirable gloves for the ladies, and summer boots
for fine gentlemen." The skins of Jews *were* made into
leather in Hitler's Germany. Such was the consequence
of one portion of the population enslaving and
dehumanizing another portion of the population. What
are the future consequences of exploiting women?
Recent history tells us that the realization of
Charnas's extreme vision is certainly not impossible.
        The ideas of Bruno Bettelheim, a survivor of
Hitler's death camps, shed light upon the pathological
society Alldera flees. Her life in the Holdfast surely
conforms to his definition of an "extreme situation":
"Characterizing this situation were its shattering
impact on the individual, for which he was totally
unprepared; its inescapability; the expectation that
the situation would last for an undetermined period,
potentially for a lifetime; the fact that, throughout
its entirety, one's very life would be in jeopardy at
every moment; and the fact that one was powerless to
protect oneself"[9] Both male and female Holdfasters are
overpowered by the Seniors; they are faced with a
lifetime of inescapable exploitation; they are
powerless to protect themsleves against rape and death.
        Another of Bettelheim's comments, his thoughts
about childhood schizophrenia, are also especially

----

[8]Marilyn French, *The Bleeding Heart* (New York: Summit
Books, 1980), p. 259. Further references will be
followed by BH and page number.
[9]Bruno Bettelheim, *Surviving and Other Essays* (New York:
Knopf, 1979), p. 115. Further references will be
followed by B and page number.

pertinent to life in the Holdfast:

> . . . the youngster who develops childhood
> schizophrenia seems to feel about himself
> and about his life exactly as the
> concentration camp prisoner felt about
> his: deprived of hope, and totally at the
> mercy of destructive irrational forces
> bent on using him for their goals,
> irrespective of his. . . . To develop
> childhood schizophrenia, it is sufficient
> that the infant is convinced that his life
> is run by insensitive, irrational, and
> overwhelming powers, who have total
> control over his existence and do not
> value it. For the normal adult to develop
> schizophrenia-like reactions, this
> actually has to be true, as it was in the
> German concentration camps. . . . In
> addition, specific events, different for
> each child, had convinced these children
> that they were threatened by total
> destruction all of the time, and that no
> personal relations offered any protection
> or emotional relief" (B. pp. 116-117).

The children who reside in the "boy house" and in the kit pits *are* always at the mercy of destructive irrational forces bent on using them for their own goals. The adult Holdfasters who control these institutions do not value the lives of their young charges. And, as we have seen, children and adults are threatened by destruction all of the time. They do not (with the exception of Bek) know their parents; their sexual relationships are tainted by brutality.

Thus, *Walk* is a fantasy which shares characteristics of past -- and potential future -- atrocious human acts. Although women's present reality is not analogous to the "extreme situation" depicted in the novel, as we all know, women are treated with prejudice, contempt, and malice. Efforts to deprive women of the right to be full contributors to every aspect of life are all too familiar and too numerous to mention here. Yet, happily, in reality -- and in fiction -- women are becoming something other than wives, mothers, and assistants to powerful men. Like Alldera, they wish to develop their talents to the

fullest possible extent.
      And, like Alldera, some women have positive
reasons for having hope in their lives. Alldera seizes
an opportunity to flee the Holdfast; some women have
the pleasure of knowing that when they approach their
house yard gate, they are not walking to the end of
their world.

Motherlines

      Some people may judge *Motherlines* to be morally
repugnant. Not everyone will welcome a novel which
depicts interracial lesbianism among women who mate
with horses. The first way of approaching this book,
then, is to understand why these potentially disturbing
plot elements are present.
      The novel obviously portrays an alternative to the
prevailing patriarchal culture. Gerard Klein reminds
us that the science fiction genre itself is one such
cultural alternative: ". . . not counting the as yet
unrecognized contribution by women, SF is one of the
three or four important subcultures which have been
geographically and socially 'deterritorialized' -- i.e.
which have come about Outside the prevailing culture.
As long as there is a prevailing culture, and in
consequence the wretched of that culture, such
subcultures will be born. . . . Culture, it is well
known, cannot be taught and cannot be decreed; it must
be created."[10] In *Motherlines*, Alldera literally ventures
geographically and socially outside the Holdfast's
sphere of influence. She enters the subculture the
Motherline tribes where women are no longer the
wretched of a prevailing patriarchal culture. There is
a simple reason which allows for the creation of a
culture where women dominate all aspects of society:
Alldera's new world does not include men.
      Charnas explains why *Motherlines* lacks male
characters:

----

[10]Gerard Klein, "A Petition by Agents of the Dominant
Culture for the Dismissal of Science Fiction," *Science-
Fiction Studies*, 7 (1980), 122.

I did not know until I had begun writing
that in this sequel there would be no male
characters at all. The decision to
exclude men was not dispassionate and
political. I tried to write them in; I
wanted to do more of what came fairly
easily. No matter what I wrote, men would
not fit. Every scene they entered went
dead. . . . I was terrified to discover
that leaving men out altogether was going
to be 'right' for the new book (AWA. p.
105).

In her introduction to *Women of Wonder*, Pamela Sargent
illustrates that what Charnas considers "right" is
usually judged to be definitely wrong. Sargent
stresses that the absence of male characters provokes
negative reactions: "[Russ's] 'When It Changed' won the
Nebula Award. . . . Yet it was severely criticized in
some science fiction publications. It is a bit odd
that readers should feel threatened by a story in which
well-characterized, likeable women get along without
men, when there is such an abundance of science fiction
in which well-characterized, likeable men get along
without women."[11] Even though it is possible to respect
the younger males' vitality and robustness in the face
of the horror of their entire culture, most of the men
in *Walk* are far from likeable.

Alldera describes what she has endured in the
Holdfast: "While you [members of the Motherline tribes]
rode and hunted and hugged each other here, men beat me
and starved me, a man threw me down on my back in the
mud and fucked me and made me eat dirt to remind me how
much power he had over me."[12] Yet, despite the men's
behavior, readers of *Walk* do not balk at their
presence. Because it does not exclude men, *Walk* -- a
novel that describes a brutal rape scene and the
aforementioned notion that women's flesh should be used
to solve a food shortage -- is less threatening than

----

[11]Pamela Sargent, *Women of Wonder* (New York: Random
House, 1975), p. liii.
[12]Suzy Mckee Charnas, *Motherlines*, (New York: Berkley,
1978), p. 93. Further references will be followed by M
and page number.

Marleen Barr

Motherlines.
    I believe this is true because the media routinely
saturates us with images of woman as victim. Rape --
the brutalization of women -- has become a routine and
"acceptable" aspect of our lives. A fictitious picture
of lesbians who do not reproduce in the usual way is
not as readily accepted. Because women are currently
so wretched that their degradation is commonplace, new
cultural values must be created. *Motherlines*, Charnas's
feminist utopian vision, can facilitate the creation of
such a new nonsexist culture. After experiencing the
novel, readers should feel the impetus to create
alternatives to a society where the violent treatment
of women is a normal, albeit unfortunate, occurrence.
Readers must realize that the novel's portrayal of
lesbians who enjoy sex with mutual consent and dignity,
of women who must mate with their horses because of
biological necessity, is less shocking than the scene
in *Walk* where an enslaved Alldera is raped and forced
to swallow dirt. Marilyn French's Dolores explains why
most readers will not reach such a realization about
Motherlines. They might see Charnas in the following
light: "But a woman who protests . . . a woman who
blames men or male society for anything, who complains,
is seen as a nut, a freak, an aggressor, humorless,
petty-minded, a shrew, a virago, a castrator, an
amazon, a ballbuster. Yes" (BH. p. 258). In the
following two examples, the text of *Motherlines* defends
itself: First, Nenisi, a black Riding Woman, states
that her society's reproductive methods is a logical
and superior alternative to women's experience in the
Holdfast:

> They [women who survived the "Wasting"]
> perfected the changes the labs had bred
> into them so that no men were needed. Our
> seed, when ripe, will start growing
> without merging with male seed because it
> already has its full load of traits from
> the mother. The lab men used a certain
> fluid to start this growth. So do we.
> [They use horse semen.] Simple and clean,
> compared to rape in the Holdfast (M. p.
> 74).

Or rape in our society. And, secondly, another Riding
Woman explains that, in her opinion, voluntarily mating

with a horse is an acceptable alternative to enduring
the degradation of being forced to mate with a man:

> The stud horse doesn't attack anyone, he
> means no harm, no abuse or degradation.
> He's innocent. He has to be led and
> coaxed and trained to do his part with our
> help. It's nothing at all like a man
> overpowering a fem just to show her who's
> master (M. p. 103).

These passages illustrate that the society of the
Motherline tribes is far more humane, far less brutal
and exploitative, than our prevailing American
culture's treatment and depiction of women.

The peculiar portrayal of sexuality in *Motherlines*
is not a solitary literary phenomenon created in
generic isolation. Rather, the novel shares the
concerns of other works which are a part of the recent
wave of feminist utopian science fiction: Joanna Russ's
The Female Man, Marge Piercy's *Woman on the Edge of Time*,
and Catherine Madsen's "Commodore Bork and the
Compost," for examples. In "Recent Feminist Utopias"
Russ explains why this literature is characterized by
sexual permissiveness:

> Classless, without government,
> ecologically minded with a strong feeling
> for the natural world, quasi-tribal in
> feeling and quasi-family in structure, the
> societies of these stories are sexually
> permissive -- in terms I suspect many
> contemporary male readers might find both
> unspectacular and a little baffling, but
> which would be quite familiar to the
> radical wing of the feminist movement
> since the point of the permissiveness is
> not to break taboos but to separate
> sexuality from questions of ownership,
> reproduction, and social structure. . . .
> *Woman on the Edge of Time* is reproductively
> the most inventive of the group [of the
> feminist utopian novels Russ discusses]
> with bisexuality . . . as the norm,
> exogenetic birth, triads of parents of
> both sexes caring for children, and all
> three parents nursing infants. Exclusive

> homosexuality . . . is an unremarkable
> idiosyncracy. . . . 'Commodore Bork' is
> cheerful about homosexuality,
> heterosexuality, promiscuity, and a
> reproductive technique which allows one
> woman to have a baby 'with' another;
> everybody parents.[13]

When set in the context of its own generic ilk, the
portrayal of sexuality in *Motherlines* is unremarkably
idiosyncratic. Russ's essay includes a succinct comment
which should be directed toward those readers who
cannot accept the novel's portrayal of lesbianism and
separatism: "I believe that the separatism [in feminist
utopian science fiction] is primary, and that the
authors are not subtle in their reasons for creating
separatist utopias: if men are kept out of these
societies, it is because men are dangerous. They also
hog the good things of this world" (R. p. 77). Yes.
The Riding Women continually state that they are afraid
of the danger posed by Holdfast men. For example,
Nenisi tells Alldera that "there are no men at all. . .
. None. You're safe" (M. p. 36). The Riding Women
rightfully exclude men because their society is far
superior to the prevailing situation in the Holdfast.
In fact, it is fair to say that in many ways the
society of the Motherline tribes is better than our
own.
　　The novel's alternative view of childbirth -- an
alternative whose positive effects on the mother form a
marked contrast to impersonal American hospitals --
exemplifies this point. Here are Adrienne Rich's
comments about giving birth "in the hands of the male
medical technology":

> The hierarchal atmosphere of the hospital,
> the definition of childbirth as a medical
> emergency, the fragmentation of body from
> mind, were the environment in which we
> gave birth, with or without analgesia. The
> only female presence were nurses, whose

----

[13]Joanna Russ, "Recent Feminist Utopias," in *Future
Females*, p. 76. Further references will be followed by
R and page number.

> training and schedules precluded much
> female tenderness. (I remember the
> gratitude and amazement I felt waking in
> the 'recovery room' after my third
> delivery to find a young student nurse
> holding my hand.) The experience of lying
> half-awake in a barred crib in a labor
> room with other women moaning in a drugged
> condition, where 'no one comes' except to
> give a pelvic examination or give an
> injection, is a class experience of
> alienated childbirth. The loneliness, the
> sense of abandonment, of being imprisoned,
> powerless, and depersonalized is the chief
> collective memory of women who have given
> birth in American hospitals.[14]

The mother, then, is confined within an environment controlled by men where she is friendless and helpless, where she routinely does not receive support from other women. In contrast, Alldera certainly does not feel alienated when she gives birth in the Riding Women's totally female world:

> A person with long, shining black hair was
> crouching between Alldera's legs. She put
> out her hands and something dropped into
> them. Another leaned in and carefully
> pinched the last of the blood down the
> cord. Alldera was astonished at the
> simplicity of what they did, their calm .
> . . . People came and put their faces
> against Alldera's steaming face . . . she
> thought fiercely each time one of them
> approached her, I love you forever for
> this (M. p. 34).

For Alldera, childbirth is not a medical emergency which is controlled by a male medical hierarchy. She does not feel lonely and powerless at the center of a group of women who stress the importance of offering

----

[14]Adrienne Rich, *Of Woman Born* (New York: W.W. Norton, 1976), p. 176. Further references will be followed by OWB and page number.

her their support. When Alldera's fictional experience
is compared to the reality Rich describes, the fiction
is clearly superior to the fact of giving birth in an
American hospital.

However, although *Motherlines* improves upon our own
society, Charnas has appropriately not created a
perfect utopia. Tribes of flawless women would falsely
exalt females, place them high upon undeserved
pedestals. Like all people, the women of the
Motherline tribes have their faults, quarrels, and
petty jealousies. When Alldera joins a tribal family,
all of its members do not welcome her according to an
expected open and nurturing feminine fashion. Sheel
Torrinor is just plain impolite and antagonistic.
Nenisi explains, "Good manners are not among the
Torrinor traits. Like me, Sheel is of your family. I
hope you can stand her" (M. p. 39). Hence as in *Walk*,
we are reminded that all women do not treat each other
well simply because they are women. On three occasions
Alldera goes so far as to observe that her new life
shares some of the characteristics of the Holdfast (M.
pp. 42, 56, 123). Such unpleasantness in the world
beyond the Holdfast might be disappointing; some
readers might wish that the members of a feminist
society were without fault. Alldera shares this wish:
"She had wanted the women to be perfect, and they were
not" (M. p. 99).

Since each undesirable trait is passed down
through the Motherline from generation to generation,
these women can never rectify their personal and
physical imperfections. Nenisi Connor continually
complains about her aching teeth; all of the Connors
always have had -- and always will have -- aching
teeth. Because genetic change does not occur when one
generation of Riding Women gives way to another,
Alldera is invited to join a tribal family with the
hope that her daughter, Sorrel, will be the founder of
a new Motherline. Yet, despite the enthusiasm about
Sorrel's potential to provide reproductive diversity,
the tribes' generational continuity is not without its
positive aspects. The individual woman receives the
support of other women who resemble her in addition to
the support of "share mothers" who are not related to
her. No woman is ignorant of the characteristics of
her ancestors; no woman is isolated from other women.
"Self songs" celebrate the achievements of *all* the
women's lives.

The novel, then, emphasizes women's culture. Self songs are sung proudly and openly; there are no men to stifle these female voices: "Here a voice rose in song, there another. The members of each Motherline sang all the self songs of the past generation of their line. The singing of each Motherline unfurled like a banner against the paling sky" (M. p. 173). Hence, the Riding Women are female artists and their songs are created in opposition to the usual repression of women's creativity. As they sing words which describe their lives, they exemplify the notions of French feminist critic Helene Cixous. She says, "Woman must write herself: must write about women and bring women to writing, from which they have been driven away as violently as from their bodies -- for the same reasons, by the same laws, with the same fatal goal. Woman must put herself into the text -- as into the world and into history -- by her own movement. . . . Women should break out of the snare of silence."[15] The Riding Women -- and Charnas herself -- have successfully broken out of this snare.

Robin Lakoff's thoughts about the snare of feminine language apply to *Motherlines* as well as to *Walk to the End of the World*. In *Motherlines*, the "free fems"-- escaped female Holdfast slaves who find refuge in the Riding Women's domain -- have learned to unmask their insults. They must "be careful not to use the insulting term 'Mares' in their [the Riding Women's] hearing" (M. p. 187). In the context of the novel, "Mare" metalinguistically acquires a derogatory -- and sexual -- meaning. Hence the fems no longer speak according to Lakoff's "women's language"; their utterances are not lady-like.

Nor are many of the novel's images lady-like, even though they are definitely feminine. Here for example, is a description of the first object made by a Riding Woman that Alldera encounters: "The red was a rag knotted around the end of some sort of bundle that was wedged into the crotch of a tree" (M. p. 14). The allusion to menstruation is unmistakable. Although this pervasive aspect of a woman's life is not routinely mentioned in novels, Charnas refers to it

----

[15]Helene Cixous, "The Laugh of the Medusa," *Signs* 1 (1976), 875, 881.

Marleen Barr

directly: "Alldera sat knotting the dry fibers spread on her knee into a menstrual plug. She could not yet turn out dozens of them during a conversation without looking down at her work, as the women did; but she could make enough for her own needs" (M. p. 59). Like a fisherman mending a net, Alldera is openly doing necessary work. The Riding Women have an appropriate attitude toward menstruation; they do not veil it in myth, secrecy, or blue and white flowered, unmarked cardboard boxes.

Their attitude toward men's bodies also differs from our cultural norm: they believe the penis to be an encumbering and ridiculous organ. To Sheel, a man's "sexual organs had seemed a ludicrous dangling nuisance and hardly capable of the brutalities recounted by the escaped femmish slaves. Having everything external and crowded into the groin like that must make walking more uncomfortable for a man than riding at the gallop with unsupported, milk-full breasts would be for a plains woman" (M. p. 17). Since such an attitude is so seldom articulated, it is worthwhile to also note young Sorrel's thoughts about men's anatomy: "It [a penis] sounds silly and clumsy, like carrying a lance around with you all the time" (M. p. 259). Ironically, to these women, the penis is ludicrous and potentially dangerous. But, most importantly, they certainly do not envy it. (There are no cigar smokers in *Motherlines*.) Instead of presenting the usual phallocentric viewpoint, this novel depicts women's biological reality. Its frankness is apparent, for example, when the rawness of new mother Alldera's vagina is described after she urinates (M. p. 42). *Motherlines* does not define this female organ as an inferior version of men's genitals.

The text emphasizes that the absence of sexual violence coincides with the absence of men. The women do not rape each other. Nor do they rape the land by thrusting their presence upon it without regard for the ecological impact of their actions. Like the American Indians, the Motherline tribes respect the plains and the animals who share their environment: "We are in touch with strong currents that hold all the things and beings and forces of the plains in balance. Any woman here can be helped to find that balance. But you can't put in balance something that never belonged at all" (M. p. 170). They live freely and well in their nontechnological -- and nonsexist -- world.

I want to reiterate that their world is better
than our own. Better, even though the absence of men --
and the sexual implications of that absence -- might
make some readers uncomfortable. Such discomfort is
unreasonable. The Riding Women's sexuality is a
natural part of the balance of their world. In
contrast, Americans accept and perpetuate immoral
activities which do not belong in the balance of our
culture: portrayals of pornography and violence. A
popular magazine comments about the pervasive presence
of these elements in contemporary American life.

> In the new pornography of gore, sadistic
> movies routinely fill the screen with
> mangled and severed bodies. TV violence,
> though less graphic, is even more
> pervasive. One study says that the
> average American youth will witness 11,000
> TV murders by the time he is 14. Worse,
> scripts are customarily structured to make
> violence seem like the logical solution to
> human problems.[16]

French's Dolores voices an opinion about such violence:
"Because, she wanted to say, look at the world! Look at
the cracks, the jokes, the whistles, the pawing hands,
the rapes, the judgments, the ads, the movies, the TV,
the books, the laws, the traditions, the customs, the
economic statistics. . ." (BH. p. 257). She would
enthusiastically approve of the fact that the Riding
Women do not entertain themselves by creating violence;
Charnas does not try to entertain readers by creating a
violent text.
  It is immoral to condemn *Motherlines* while passively
accepting the violence and the sexist images of women
we routinely see on TV and movie screens. Although a
fictitious portrayal of loving -- and biologically
necessary -- sexuality is more constructive than a
nightly parade of murder victims, ironically, *Motherlines*
would never be televised in America. The presence of
two women loving each other in a text is condemned; the
presence of myriad mangled and severed female bodies on
the screen is condoned. This is wrong. Instead of

----

[16]*Time* Magazine, 22 December 1980, p. 32.

Marleen Barr

witnessing 11,000 TV murders, the average American
youth should witness 11,000 portrayals of women as
whole, useful and mature human beings. *Motherlines*
presents one such portrayal. It does not present
violence as a logical solution to human problems.
   Rather, it posits another solution, a solution
that emerges from the words of Adrienne Rich: "We do
not actually know much about what power may have meant
in the hands of strong, prepatriarchal women. We do
have guesses, longings, myths, fantasies, analogues.
We know far more about how, under patriarchy, female
possibility has been literally massacred on the site of
motherhood" (OWB. p. 13). *Motherlines* is a guess, a
longing, a fantasy, and an analogue about the power of
women who are not repressed by the patriarchy. The
novel presents a solution to those human problems that
perpetuate the repression of women: female possibility
must flourish on the site of motherhood.

   As I have said elsewhere,[17] feminist readers of
Walk and *Motherlines* might feel disgruntled by the
publication of Charnas's third novel, *The Vampire
Tapestry* (1980). It is not the promised and expected
completion to her trilogy. Those who were looking
forward to seeing Alldera triumphantly leading the
Riding Women back to establish a feminist society in
the Holdfast will be dissatisfied by *Vampire's*
departure from the first two novels' characters and
settings. Regarding the creation of a society where
men and women function together with harmony and
equality, both life and literature fall short of
utopia. We have not as yet walked to the end of the
male chauvinist world.

----

[17]See Marleen Barr, "Holding Fast to Feminism and
Moving Beyond: Suzy McKee Charnas's *The Vampire
Tapestry*," in *The Feminine Eye*, ed. Tom Staicar (New
York: Ungar, 1982), pp. 60-72.

WORLD VIEWS IN UTOPIAN NOVELS BY WOMEN

Lucy M. Freibert

Of the one hundred sixty utopian or near-utopian novels published in America between 1888 and 1900,[1] fewer than a dozen were by women, and, according to Ann J. Lane, only one -- Mary E. Bradley Lane's *Mizora* (1890) is "self-consciously feminist."[2] Even that one falls short. A truly feminist work espouses social principles and practices that would create a society free of oppression and discrimination based on sex, race, age, class, religion, and sexual orientation, thereby assuring women opportunities for personal autonomy. *Mizora*, although it purports to present a classless society, posits a money- and property-based economy, retains the concept of servants, and boasts of having eliminated dark-complexioned people because they supposedly embodied evil.

The first truly feminist work in the American utopian tradition -- *Herland*,[3] written by Charlotte Perkins Gilman in 1915 and serialized in *The Forerunner* -- did not appear in book form until 1979. Since the sixties, a number of feminist works set totally or partially in utopian worlds have emerged. Among them are *The Kin of Ata Are Waiting for You* (1971) by Dorothy Bryant, *The Dispossessed* (1974) by Ursula Le Guin, *The Female Man* (1975) by Joanna Russ, *From the Legend of Biel*

----

[1] Stuart A. Teitler, "Introduction," Mary E. Bradley Lane, *Mizora: A Prophecy* (Boston: Gregg Press, 1975), p. lx, No. 2.
[2] Ann J. Lane, "Introduction," Charlotte Perkins Gilman, *Herland* (New York: Pantheon Books, 1979), p. xix.
[3] Charlotte Perkins Gilman, *Herland* (New York: Pantheon Books, 1979). All further references will be cited in the text.

Lucy M. Freibert

(1975) by Mary Staton, *Woman on the Edge of Time* (1976) by Marge Piercy, and *The Wanderground* (1979) by Sally Miller Gearhart.[4]
It is not surprising that feminist utopian works have only recently begun to grow in number. Until the second half of the nineteenth century there was no strong feminist vision in America. And the apathy that followed the passage of the Nineteenth Amendment rapidly dissipated the nineteenth-century feminist movement, of which *Mizora* and *Herland* are outgrowths. Not until the 1947 appearance of Simone de Beauvoir's *The Second Sex* focused women's attention on the concept of personal autonomy, and almost simultaneous advances in applied science gave them more control over their reproductive lives, did numbers of women writers begin building literary utopias.
Examination of four of these works -- *Herland*, *The Dispossessed*, *Woman on the Edge of Time*, and *The Wanderground* -- in the order of their publication, reveals shared principles and discloses a pattern which is emerging in the feminist canon. The four utopias dispense with private property but provide rooms of their own for everyone. They also furnish food, clothing, education, medical care, travel, and recreation at common expense. The utopias provide community dining facilities and child-care centers, and extend parenting responsibilities to all community members. They eliminate family names to avoid the implication that children are property. All open diverse occupations to women and, perhaps most important, through community concern, eradicate the fear of rape and assault. These principles are present not only in the utopian novels under consideration but in all contemporary feminist works, including those written by men.[5]

----

[4]Dorothy Bryant, *The Kin of Ata Are Waiting for You* (New York: Random House, 1971); Ursula Le Guin, *The Dispossessed* (New York: Avon, 1974); Joanna Russ, *The Female Man* (New York: Bantam, 1975); Mary Staton, *From the Legend of Biel* (New York: Ace, 1975); Marge Piercy, *Woman on the Edge of Time* (New York: Fawcett Crest, 1976); Sally Miller Gearhart, *The Wanderground* (Watertown, Massachusetts: Persephone Press, 1979).
[5]Carol Pearson, "Women's Fantasies and Feminist

In addition to these general principles, an even
deeper relationship exists among the four works treated
here. All base their world views on organicism. Each
grows from a root metaphor of historic process which
emphasizes the systemic interdependence of the various
fragments of the social structure, and this coherence
forms a basis for optimism. As Stephen C. Pepper
points out in *World Hypotheses*, "an organic whole is
such a system that every element within it implies
every other." As the disparate elements within the
system conflict and through conflict reach new
integration, the society evolves to higher and higher
levels of perception toward the absolute. The
organicist root metaphor embodies, therefore, the idea
of a living, progressing system.[6] *Herland* is based on
the metaphor of motherhood, *The Dispossessed* on anarchy,
Woman on the Edge of Time on personhood, and *The
Wanderground* on sisterhood. Each metaphor posits a
developmental and/or interrelational process with the
potential of moving toward a new and better state. Of
particular importance in these novels is the origin of
each utopia and each utopia's ideology, government,
education, and language. The choice of organic
metaphors by women authors advocates the union of
reason and nature, rather than the domination of nature
practiced by the current male-oriented culture.

Gilman's choice of the root metaphor of motherhood
for her novel *Herland* is obviously appropriate for
conveying her serio-comic criticism of the patriarchal
western tradition. Gilman's female society has
eliminated all the ills of western culture but remains
open to possible reincorporation of men into the
structure, if experimentation shows that to be an
improvement.

The history of Herland reveals the stages of
evolution. About 2000 years before the story opens, a
volcanic eruption cut off the country's only outlet to
the sea and buried most of the male population, who
were engaged in defending the passage. Male slaves
murdered the few remaining males, the old women and the
mothers, but young women and girls then killed the male

Utopias," *Frontiers* II, No. 3, 1977, pp. 50-61.
[6]Stephen C. Pepper, *World Hypotheses* (Berkeley and Los
Angeles: University of California Press, 1942), p. 300.

slaves. The women, including the few remaining slave
women, set about farming and caring for one another.
For five or ten years, the community worked at
developing the country and themselves, and then a
miracle happened. One of the women bore a child
through parthenogenesis -- a process which produces
only female children. In ensuing years she bore four
more daughters. These five women inherited their
mother's power and, beginning at the age of twenty-
five, each bore five children. Gradually, the old
people died and only the one family, all descended from
one mother, remained. As the family increased, the
society focused on nurturing the children and
developing an ecologically balanced environment.

The social pattern or world view which evolves is
based on love and reason, and the communal ideals of
beauty, health, strength, intellect, and goodness --
"for these they prayed and worked" (p. 59). Their
religion before the catastrophe had been like the
Greeks', but gradually the women lose interest in gods
of war and plunder and center on the Mother Goddess.
In their Maternal Pantheism, God seems "an Indwelling
Spirit, . . . an immense Loving Power working steadily
out through them, toward good" (pp. 112-113, 115).
This theological organicism carries over into their
philosophy. Their ethics, based on the full perception
of evolution, shows the principle of growth and the
beauty of a wise culture: "They [have] no theory of the
essential opposition of good and evil; life to them
[is] growth; their pleasure [is] in growing, and their
duty also" (p. 102).

Since love and reason rule, politics in Herland
concentrates on preserving and improving quality of
life. The Great Over Mother of the Land and her High
Temple Counsellors comprise the guiding body. Decision
making, however, is by consensus. There are no laws
over a hundred years old, and most laws are fewer than
twenty years old. This vision of the law as organic,
rather than eternally codified, parallels the other
evolutionary aspects of the society. At one point,
when the population threatens to exceed the number
which the country can reasonably be expected to support
(three million), the community agrees that each woman
will limit her mothering power to having one child.
Similarly, the community counsels the physically or
mentally weak to suppress the maternal urge. Thus
defects of mind and body are bred out, and the family

becomes stronger and increasingly more intelligent,
innovative, imaginative, and physically beautiful. At
death each person is cremated and her remains returned
to Mother Earth.[7]
Education, geared to support their ethics,
continues a lifetime and concentrates on evolving the
intellect and the will. Those with critical and
inventive minds get the greatest attention. As a
result of lifelong engagement in acrobatics and
dancing, women of all ages are strong and agile. The
dancing is athletic, recreational, and ritualistic, and
is integral to all celebrations, pageants, and
processions.
The language is simple but expressive. Literature
for children includes simple repetitive verse and story
and the most "exquisite imaginative tales" (p. 102).
It is the work of great artists, and true to the world
around them. Literature for the adults is equally
fine; its focus is on positive relationships rather
than on the tension created by envy and jealousy as in
most national literatures. Everyone engaged in the
arts and crafts signs her works, so that others might
know whom to thank when using them.
The mothering metaphor pervades the narrative as
well as Herland's social structure. When three
American men appear in Herland, the women devise means
to learn from them everything possible about the
outside world and at the same time to protect
themselves from abuse. On the possibility that a
heterosexual society might have something to offer to
improve the quality of life and move the country closer
to absolute perfection, the Herlanders allow the
gentlest of the men to remain in Herland and permit the

----

[7]Two questions arise concerning *Herland*: first,
Gilman's advocacy of selective breeding, which would
produce the "superior race" at the expense of
"defective citizens"; second, how is it that in her
otherwise democratic society she advances an authority
figure, the Great Over Mother. The time during which
Herland was written provides the answers. The lessons
of World War I and World War II did much to undermine
American racist attitudes, but Gilman's work, after
all, was contemporary with that other flawed American
masterpiece, *The Birth of a Nation* (1915).

Lucy M. Freibert

most adventuresome woman to go to the States. In characteristically organicist fashion, the novel ends on the note of waiting -- waiting for the creation of a child by the union of man and woman in Herland and for a report from the envoy to the States.

On the surface, the utopian experience depicted in Le Guin's *The Dispossessed*, published fifty-nine years later, differs significantly from that in *Herland*. Whereas Herland emerges as the result of a cosmic eruption and a biological leap, and produces a luxurious natural culture, the utopian community in Le Guin's novel originates in social upheaval and develops in modest, though scientifically advanced, circumstances. At the core, however, the organic development of both societies results from women's power and produces conditions specifically amenable to women's needs.

One hundred seventy years before *The Dispossessed* opens, a group of anarchists, led by the philosopher Odo, arose on the planet Urras. To prevent their "wrecking the profiteering states and setting up the just society there," the Urrasti allowed Odo's one million followers to set up a colony on the moon Anarres.[8] Physical conditions on the satellite were not conducive to developing a plush existence, but the Odonians preferred a frugal life in freedom to continued stagnation in the corrupt capitalistic society of Urras. After all, did not Odo's aesthetics and ethics hold that "Excess is excremental"?

Although the Odonians were willing to live more simply, their anarchism was the "product of a very high civilization," and they determined to reproduce in Anarres equivalents of the best aspects of that civilization. They held fast to the ideal of "complex organicism." "They built the roads first, the houses second. The special resources and products of each region were interchanged continually with those of others, in an intricate process of balance: that balance of diversity which is the characteristic of life, of natural and social ecology" (p. 78). The Odonians' achievement of an organicism, given their roots in anarchy, is as much a miracle as

----

[8] Le Guin, p. 35. All further references will be cited in the text.

parthenogenesis in Herland. Leaving behind the hierarchical, codified laws of men and following Odo's organicist principles, each person concentrated on developing his or her own life to the fullest, simultaneously combining the complexity, vitality, and freedom of invention and initiative essential to Odonian ideals.

The antithetical ideals of freedom and solidarity become the touchstones of the land. Odo's principles of revolution and suffering integrate the two. Odo teaches that each person contains the spirit of revolution within. As Shevek explains the theory, "The duty of the individual is to accept rule, to be initiator of his own acts, to be responsible . . . . Revolution is our obligation: our hope of evolution" (pp. 288-9). Shevek reflects this principle when, 170 years after the founding of the settlement, he seeks to return to Urras to share his theories with specialists there. Rulag, his mother, reflects the same principle when she appears before the Council to challenge his request. Insofar as each individual lives up to his or her responsibility, change, that is, orderly growth, the central principle of nature, is assured.

Odo also teaches that suffering is the condition of living and that preventing and overcoming suffering is the goal of life. By standing together and doing what each does best, people can eliminate individual and communal suffering. Thus private and public conscience -- one's own pleasure and the respect gained from one's companions -- advance the society.

Because of the integration of the ideals of freedom and solidarity, no formal government is needed in Anarres to control the country's systems. Nevertheless, order requires that there be a center from which directives and information can be sent out: "The computers that [coordinate] the administration of things, the division of labor, the distribution of goods, and the central federatives of most of the work syndicates, [are] in Abbernay" (p. 78). This unavoidable centralization is, of course, a threat to freedom. However, the system allows for an individual to request a particular posting which he or she feels is necessary for personal development or the country's good and to refuse an appointment that seems stifling to self or ineffectual for the common good. As stated above, it is the duty of the individual to see that the system works, that the needs of the country as well as

Lucy M. Freibert

his or her own are met.
    Personal as well as professional and civic
relationships on Anarres are subject to the polarities
of freedom and solidarity. Although there is no
marriage, Odonians undertake monogamy just as they
might any other partnership:

> Partnership was a voluntarily constituted
> federation like any other. So long as it
> worked, it worked, and if it didn't work
> it stopped being. It was not an
> institution but a function. It had no
> sanction but that of private conscience
> (p. 197). . . . An Anarresti knew he had
> to be ready to go where he was needed and
> do the work that needed doing. He grew up
> knowing labor distribution as a major
> factor of life, an immediate, permanent
> social necessity; whereas conjugality was
> a personal matter, a choice that could be
> made only within the larger choice (p.
> 198).

Freedom and commitment within such a relationship are
possible on Anarres because all children are cared for
in the nursery and school. Most parents keep in touch
with their children, taking them out for meals and
recreation. In some cases, however, where one parent
or the other is deeply involved in an occupation, the
other parent might be the only one to look in on the
child. Shevek knew this experience, as he was cared
for mainly by his father, while his mother, an
engineer, was posted elsewhere.
    In the nursery and learning centers the children
are educated according to their abilities. They are
taught to share and to be responsible for examining
critically everything they are taught. No sexual
distinctions enter into their educations.
Consequently, women are represented equally with men
among the most advanced scientists in the society:
Mitis is the senior physicist; Gavarab, the greatest
cosmologist; and Rulag, an engineer. In addition to
splendid academic preparation, children are well
trained physically, especially in the martial arts.
They are carefully prepared for sexual ease with each
other. To achieve this state, they have sexual
experiences with their peers of both sexes from their

earliest years. Education in respect for the other
person's sexual needs and preferences eliminates rape
and allows real freedom to enjoy copulation or abstain
from it.

The uniqueness of each person on Anarres is
symbolized by the name given at birth. The name,
created by the central computer, will never be
duplicated for anyone else. Family names are
unnecessary for identification, thus eliminating the
sense of ownership which a family name can convey.
Everyone is seen, and expected to act, as an autonomous
being.

The assignment of a unique name is only one
reflection of the Odonian concern with the relationship
between people and language. When the Odonians left
Urras for Anarres, they left behind the language of
their ancestors and in true anarchist fashion,
developed a rationally-structured language of their
own. Clumsy at first, the language achieved graceful
precision through the evolution of literature.

Since the root metaphor underlying *The Dispossessed*
is anarchy, the society presented is constantly in a
state of flux, evolving toward perfection. The
internal motivation for the narrative lies in Shevek's
efforts to correct the corruption that he perceives in
the publication process controlled by Sabul, an envious
older colleague. Shevek's efforts to combine the
Sequency and Simultaneity theories into a General
Temporal Theory and to share the result with other
specialists take him to Urras, where, in the midst of
the capitalist culture, he works out the organic
temporal theory and spreads the knowledge of his
achievement with the help of local anarchists.

This organicist philosophy pervades the book to
the very end. Having achieved his immediate goal,
Shevek returns to Anarres and on the trip back learns
that his act of anarchy has sparked activity at home,
creating the possibility of a disruptive reception upon
his arrival in the Port of Abbernay. Ironically, but
appropriately, Shevek's precarious state inspires one
of the Urrasti space crew to disembark with him in
order to share the evolutionary freedom that Anarres
represents. Thus, the finale of *The Dispossessed*, like
that of *Herland*, preserves the ongoing nature of the
organicist metaphor and supports the belief that risk
generates growth.

The utopia depicted in Marge Piercy's novel, *Woman*

Lucy M. Freibert

on the Edge of Time, is particularly characteristic of
the twentieth century. It is the psychological
projection of Consuelo Comacho Ramos, a Chicana mental
patient so frustrated by the treatment received inside
and outside the hospital that she generates a world in
which to find solidarity and advice. So real does
Connie's fantasy world become that when one of its
citizens visits her, the body heat left on a kitchen
chair is detected by an unexpected visitor from the
real world.

The controlling metaphor underlying Connie's
utopia is personhood: the growth of the culture
resembling that of a human being's maturation. This
choice is not surprising, since Connie's life has been
one of triple oppression--woman, ethnic minority, and
mental patient -- she has been made to feel more like
an object than a human being. Her utopia is,
therefore, compensatory. Like that of Anarres, it is
futuristic, being laid in Mattapoisett, Massachusetts,
in 2137. Connie's utopian vision emphasizes one
particular culture, that of the Wamponaug Indians. The
inhabitants, however, are racially mixed and range
widely in skin tone as a result of the decision of the
grand council "to breed a high proportion of darker-
skinned people and to mix the genes well throughout the
population" so that racism will never develop again.[9]
Some of the envisioned inhabitants of Connie's utopia
are versions of the people whom she has known most
intimately in New York, especially her daughter and her
former husbands. The major difference between the two
sets of people is that every person in Mattapoisett is
loved and respected by others, while people in the real
world are only too frequently despised, neglected, and
mistreated.

The sense of personal value enjoyed by the
inhabitants of Mattapoisett is conveyed in numerous
ways. One of the most striking is the non-sexist
structure and content of the language. The third
person pronominal forms *he* and *she* are replaced by the
word *person*, the shortened form *per* is used for
possessive and objective cases, and *p'self* replaces the
reflexive. Masculine roots and derivatives are simply

----

[9]Piercy, p. 103-4. All further references will be
cited in the text.

-76-

eliminated from the vocabulary.

The high priority given to personal development in Mattapoisett extends from birth to death. Population is carefully controlled. A new child is begun only when someone has died. Children are developed at the brooder, an electronically monitored building in which fetuses are scientifically produced and developed within perfect womb conditions. At birth, the children are placed in the care of three mothers with whom there is no genetic connection. The mothers may be any combination of men and women, but they must have expressed the desire to mother together. Luciente, Connie's contact person, explains the origin of this arrangement:

> "It was part of women's long revolution. When we were breaking all the old hierarchies. Finally there was that one thing we had to give up too, the only power we ever had, in return for no more power for anyone. The original production: the power to give birth. 'Cause as long as we were biologically enchained, we'd never be equal. And males would never be humanized to be loving and tender. So we all became mothers. Every child has three. To break the nuclear bonding" (p. 105).

This rational approach to population development at the expense of so great a sacrifice on the part of women raises one of the problems to be discussed later.

The emphasis placed on the person in Mattapoisett is reflected in the series of names which the individual may have. At birth, each child is given a name, but after the rites of passage at the end of mothering, the child selects a name of per own, based on per initiation experience. Some people change names several times in life without fear of losing identity, so secure are they within the community. This security results from interpersonal concern.

While personhood is important, so is the concept of community. Far more time is spent on working out interpersonal relationships than on anything else. For example, if two people have a difficulty or encounter jealousy, the whole community meets for a consultation to help them resolve the issue. Because of the

Lucy M. Freibert

importance of community, the problem of evil is
generally looked upon in terms of "power and greed --
taking from other people their food, their liberty,
their health, their land, their customs, their pride"
(p. 139). Promiscuous copulation is considered evil
only when it involves pain or is not invited. Those
who offend others by violence are dealt with lovingly
but firmly. Whether the act of violence is intended or
not, the miscreant is treated and healed. Since all
are trained in martial arts, physical violence is rare.
However, if rape or murder does occur, the offending
individual is treated. If the crime is repeated, the
person is executed. In a loving community, this use of
capital punishment seems extreme. But to the
Mattapoisett community, the logic is simple: "Second
time someone uses violence, we give up. We don't want
to watch each other or to imprison each other. We
aren't willing to live with people who choose to use
violence. We execute them" (p. 209).
     Government in Mattapoisett operates on a
grassroots structure. Each township has planners whose
ages range from sixteen upward. Many planners are
women. Members are chosen by lot and serve for a year
-- three months with the old representative, six months
alone, and three months with the successor. Planners
are limited to five-minute speeches in each discussion:
"anything person can't say in five minutes, person is
better off not saying" (p. 150). The Animal Advocate
and the Earth Advocate are chosen by dream. Lots are
drawn among those who dream that they are called to
these positions. Regional representatives are chosen
by the township. There is no final authority in the
country; decisions are made by consensus, and the
winners feed the losers and give them presents (pp.
150-154).
     As in Herland and Anarres, the education of
children is the responsibility of the whole community.
Children learn to read early. They play, work, and
study at their mothers' sides. Special effort is made
to develop their knowledge of their own states of
consciousness and feelings. They are taught to control
blood and pulse pressure; thus, they have the power to
keep their bodies healthy and develop them to their
fullest potential. Sexual play, as in Anarres, begins
early and is bisexual. After "naming day," the child
is separated from the mothers and lives as an adult.
Each of these steps is part of the maturation process,

evolving toward fuller personhood.

The utopian world of *Woman on the Edge of Time* is as realistic as those of *Herland* and *Anarres* in recognizing the need to ward off the enemy. Battles are fought at a distance from the villages and persons take turns serving in defense. Having learned from her Mattapoisett community that defending one's self is a part of being, Connie instigates her own war on the New York doctors who have been experimenting with her and her peers. Realizing that she will suffer in return, she sees that retaliation is something she can bear with dignity, knowing that she is counteracting the violence which the doctors, and society in general, have perpetrated against her very being. This decision indicates the maturity to which she has come through her experiences in 2137.

Although Sally Gearhart's *The Wanderground* bears the subtitle *Stories of the Hill Women*, it reads like a novel -- a novel having a group of women rather than only one woman at its center. It is set in a post-nuclear period, when the territory surrounding the City threatens sterility to those who choose to inhabit it. Men, who fear impotency, stay within the city walls. But many women, frustrated at every turn by the urban society, leave the City gradually and set up a nurturing, healing, loving community in the hills. Their number grows steadily, as the male-dominated society makes life increasingly unbearable for women, especially lesbians. Finally, a series of events precipitates a mass exodus. An ultra-conservative wave overtakes the City. Men in all walks of life step up their harassment of women on the job. Groups of men hunt working women down at night, and the women never appear at work again. As the hunts multiply, larger numbers of women leave the City. Some among the Hill Women return to the City and live disguised as men in order to protect their less sturdy sisters. They help those who want to escape to the hills, and they report urban trends or threats. Other women watch at outposts along the border, warning of the approach of anyone other than a woman.

The Hill community is built around the concept of sisterhood, the root metaphor which structures the novel. The community is composed of predominantly dark-skinned women, who dedicate themselves entirely to the bond of love, a bond modeled on the example of nature. The women see themselves as part of the cosmic system, as sisters to the mineral, plant, and animal worlds. They learn secrets from these forms of being. From the earth itself they extract energy by physical contact and controlled breathing. With trees and plants they exchange energy, again, by breathing. They learn to converse with animals through signs and facial expressions.

For the women who come to the Wanderground as adults, this bonding serves as therapy for overcoming the oppression which they have experienced in the City. For younger women the bonding provides an expansive environment, free of fear, in which they can develop previously undreamed-of powers. This freedom from fear gives the women courage to trust the *lonth* (the subconscious), allowing it to do things that the conscious self could never effect. They learn mental telepathy and the power of mental healing. They learn to move objects through space, to produce glow lobes (free-floating lights), to levitate and fly through the air (wind-riding), and to swim long distances under water, even through underground caverns. In a word, they become one with the pulsations of nature; they live a truly organic life. The importance of discovering and developing these natural powers lies not in the achievement, but rather in the use to which the powers are put -- helping their sisters to enjoy a full and happy life, far superior to what any of them has ever known before. Perhaps the most valuable power is that of "enfoldment," a spiritual transmission of energy and love that provides strength on which a person may draw during any mental or physical crisis.

Ordinary business of the community, such as work rotation and protection, is carried out by the Long Dozen, representatives from all the areas of the Wanderground. Their meetings, held each evening, may be attended in either the "hard self" (physical presence) or "soft self" (spirit only). Major decisions are made by consensus of all inhabitants brought together in a "gatherstretch." One other time that all the members of the community assemble is when a woman asks to be "implanted" so that she may have a child. That ritual, held in the Cella, a conch-like space in the center of the earth, exposes the person being implanted to an intense blast of "earthbreath" which produces parthenogenesis. In some instances, only the enfoldment of the sisterhood enables a person to survive the experience.

Education, designed to produce the autonomous
person -- the freestanding self -- must introduce all
to a new kind of love, one which begins by centering
the self, one which never says to another, "I cannot
live without you."[10] While each child has a
"learntogether" with whom she develops a strong
relationship, she does not become dependent on the
person. Since each child has seven mothers,
exclusiveness and jealousy are rare.
    The community recognizes that both adults and
children need education. Adults learn to transcend the
past and to use the memory of its harshness to build
solidarity with their sisters. Jacqua's experience is
typical: "She tried to recall the lessons from the
remember rooms: the stories, the mind pictures, the
pain of some not-so-ancient days when the men owned all
things, even the forests and hills. 'It is too
simple,' she recited dutifully to herself, 'to condemn
them all or to praise all of us. But for the sake of
earth and all she holds, that simplicity must be our
creed'" (p. 2). This insight into the guilt shared by
the sexes and the need for radical change is typical of
the profound truths that *The Wanderground* treats.
Rationale is not often spelled out, for conditions have
surpassed the point of explanation. For those who have
pondered the issues of power and injustice, no
explanations are necessary. For those who do not
already see, none would suffice.
    Children of the Wanderground must learn the
physical and mental skills that build harmony with
nature and their companions. The physical and mental
skills are learned through instruction and practice.
The social skills are taught through the study of
women's history. Understanding the past helps explain
current practices. Sessions in the learning centers
and memory rooms, where the children listen to women's
stories, are accompanied by the technique of
"shielding," that is, special counseling which helps
the children avoid possible ill effects of hearing some
of the personal accounts.
    The intuition required of the reader of *The
Wanderground* is challenged to the fullest through the

----

[10]Gearhart, p. 2. All further references will be cited
in the text.

introduction of the logical, if somewhat primitive, vocabulary. One is expected to learn from the context the meaning of such words as "lonth," "shielding," "implantment," "gatherstretch," etc. The use of this vocabulary and the demands which it places on the reader achieve two effects. They force the reader to experience the shock of living in an unfamiliar culture, and they allow the reader to stretch the imagination, to see by contrast the differences between a society concerned with gaining power (the real world) and one concerned with loving (the Wanderground).

Reviewing these novels illustrates that starting with organic metaphors such as motherhood, anarchy, personhood, and sisterhood, integrated communities can be conceived in which women do acquire a sense of autonomy. In that regard, the world views implied by these works inspire hope. The illustrations also insist that certain basic principles relating to women must be incorporated in any truly just society. The inclusion of such feminist principles in each of the models examined justifies their classification as utopias of reconstruction, that is, utopias which present "a vision of a reconstituted environment which is better adapted to the nature and aims of the human beings who dwell within it than the actual one."[11]

The most obvious question to be asked about the choice of root metaphors for the works is why the authors have chosen organicism as a model. After all, biological organicism has been used for centuries to keep women in their place. What reason is there to believe that another organicist structure will prove any more beneficial?

One answer seems to be that, although biological organicism has been used traditionally as a limiting force to maintain power over women, in these novels, the organic concepts have been combined with reason to liberate not only women but all people in the society. Whereas in the past men have harnessed the natural powers of the earth in order to gain control over both nature and weaker members of the human race, in these novels men and women work together studying nature's laws and learning to cooperate with them to expand both

----

[11]Lewis Mumford, *The Story of Utopias* (New York: The Viking Press, 1962), p. 26.

human consciousness and universal potential. The emphasis on the reasonableness and justice of actions and policies within the utopias is ultimately the saving grace of each culture.

The second question, again a very basic one, deals with risk-taking, a characteristic of the autonomous person. The communities delineated in these four novels evoke a sense of security and solidarity which develops confidence. As a result, the women characters readily engage in risk-taking ventures. In *Herland* this willingness to risk goes only so far as to take in one male and to send out one investigator. In *The Dispossessed*, women place mothering and mating second (or lower) to careers in science and technology, risking thereby the total loss of the mothering trait in the long-term evolutionary process. In *Woman on the Edge of Time*, women surrender the exclusivity of mothering. Moreover, their willingness to risk includes going into mortal combat and deliberately counseling violence as a means of achieving one's ends. In *The Wanderground*, while justified anger is dealt with in a theraputic manner and channeled wisely, the use of violence in relating to men is ever present. Admittedly, risk-taking is essential to growth; the question is how far women in the real world want that risk taking to carry them into areas of violence, a tactic which has led to useless slaughter and oppression for women and other cultural minorities.

Three questions arise regarding Piercy's work. Since her protagonist, Connie, rebels against theraputic control in the real world, how can she condone behavior modification in the imagined utopia? Moreover, since the basic metaphor of *Woman on the Edge of Time* is that of personhood, how can Piercy suggest capital punishment as a response to a second major offense? Third, is it necessary, or wise, for women to give up biological motherhood, as is done in Mattapoisett, in order to put men and women on an equal footing in controlling human life within the community? As Margaret Mead and others have pointed out repeatedly, gaining control of human life, particularly reproduction, has been the goal of men for centuries. Recurring efforts to create life by scientific means obviously reflect this fact. Piercy's answers are not totally satisfying.

Ultimately, in all areas of questioning regarding *Herland*, *The Dispossessed*, *Woman on the Edge of Time*, and

Lucy M. Freibert

The Wanderground, the issue at hand is power over life.
Again, the initial question must be raised: can an
organicist structure be found which will eliminate the
risk of a new kind of oppression for women? The answer
seems to be yes -- but only if reason and justice
prevail.

Reprinted from the *Journal of Popular Culture*, 17, No. 1.

THE HEAVENLY UTOPIA OF ELIZABETH STUART PHELPS

Carol Farley Kessler

Elizabeth Stuart Phelps, for those not familiar with her, lived from 1844 to 1911. She was raised in Andover, Massachusetts, where her father taught at Andover Theological Seminary, an institution founded in 1807 to maintain a conservative trinitarian theology against Harvard's unitarian innovation. Phelps's mother, also an author, died when her daughter was eight years old. The latter assumed her mother's name sometime between eight and twelve years.

Between 1868 and 1887, Phelps published three fantasies depicting a heavenly afterlife.[1] Many have considered these purely consolatory in type, but I should like to stress their utopian function.[2] Of

----

[1] Elizabeth Stuart Phelps [Ward], *The Gates Ajar* (1868; rpt. Cambridge: Harvard University Press, 1964); *Beyond the Gates* (Boston: Houghton, Mifflin Co., 1883); *The Gates Between* (Boston: Houghton, Mifflin Co., 1887). Although Phelps was adamant that subsequent *Gates* books not be advertised as sequels to the first, we can best examine them as a series because the books of 1883 and 1887 successively amplify her theme of Heaven as utopia. On the subject of sequels, see Phelps to Francis Jackson Garrison, 26 July 1883, The Beinecke Rare Book and Manuscript Library, Yale University; on dramatization see Phelps [Ward] to Henry Oscar Houghton, 15 May 1895 and 23 November [1895].
[2] For interpretation as consolation literature, see Fred Lewis Pattee, *A History of American Literature since 1870* (New York: Appleton Century, 1915), pp. 222-23; Arthur Hobson Quinn, *American Fiction: An Historical and Critical Survey* (New York: Appleton Century, 1936), pp. 194-95; Mary Angela Bennett, *Elizabeth Stuart Phelps*

Carol Farley Kessler

course a distinct problem arises when a writer casts
utopia into a heavenly afterlife, for one must die
first to qualify for the utopian existence -- a
precondition that certainly constitutes a deterrent to
social change. For the nineteenth-century author, the
vision of a heavenly utopia thus suggests ambivalence,
for on the one hand she chose a convention whereby she
might express iconoclastic views and social criticism,
while on the other, by locating her solution in a
heavenly afterlife, she indicated pessimism about
accomplishing social change. But for the twentieth-
century student, these fantasies of a heavenly
afterlife provide insight into what one woman hoped
might come to be, and what she perceived women to lack.
    Antedating most utopian writing in the United
States by some two decades, Phelps anticipated the need
to question current social changes. More than social
structure or technological power, her utopian vision
stressed the possibility of achieved human potential --
a condition in which women might fulfill themselves and
find a haven. She attempted to resolve the problems of
family structure by imagining reformed husbands and
fathers, who were required to participate in
housekeeping and child-rearing. Such changes would

(Philadelphia: University of Pennsylvania Press, 1939),
ch. 5; Perry D. Westbrook, *Acres of Flint: Writers of Rural
New England, 1870-1900* (Washington, D.C.: Scarecrow
Press, 1951), p. 15; Ann Douglas, "Heaven Our Home:
Consolation Literature in the Northern United States,
1830-1880," *American Quarterly* 26 (1974): 496-515; J. D.
Hart, *The Popular Book* (New York, 1950), ch. 7; *Notable
American Women* (1974), s.v. "Ward, Elizabeth Stuart
Phelps," by Beatrice K. Hofstadter; E. S. Phelps,
Chapters from a Life, pp. 94-130; H. S. Smith,
Introduction to *The Gates Ajar*, pp. v-xxxlii. For
interpretation as fulfillment, see Claude R. Flory,
Economic Criticism in American Fiction, 1792-1900
(Philadelphia: University of Pennsylvania Press, 1936),
p. 232; Christine Stansell, "Elizabeth Stuart Phelps: A
Study in Rebellion," *Massachusetts Review* 13 (1972):
239-56; Douglas; Barbara Welter, "The Feminization of
American Religion: 1800-1860" in *Dimity Convictions: The
American Woman in the Nineteenth Century* (Athens, Ohio,
1976), p. 137.

release to a woman energy for the pursuit of her own needs as well.

The first of her fantasies, *The Gates Ajar*, appeared in 1868. The "consolation" label fits this work more than it does her later fantasies. Begun in 1864, the book established her literary career. One impetus may have been her personal loss of a suitor at the battle of Antietam. But even more, the national impact of Civil War carnage sparked her concern. Phelps wrote that she wanted to comfort "the bereaved wife, mother, sister, and widowed girl"; that she thought of "the women the war trampled down, without a choice or protest; the patient, limited, domestic women, who thought little but loved much, and loving, had lost all."[3] She felt "prevailing beliefs" had little to say that could help an "afflicted woman" since "creeds and commentaries and sermons were made by men" (Chapters, p. 98). Although she then disclaimed sympathy with any "movement for the . . . needs of women as a class," nonetheless her own experience and her recognition of other women's needs did inform *The Gates Ajar* (Chapters, p. 99).

More important than the book's consolatory impact is its implicit social criticism. A minister's widow, Winifred Forceythe, is the potent and successful attendant to the needs of bereaved woman and man. That Phelps unreservedly gave to a woman the power usually invested in men stands in clear contrast to the inferior status accorded Andover women she knew.[4] This feminist theme, couched in conventional beliefs in the existence of a Benevolent Male Diety and Heavenly Afterlife, must have appealed to politically powerless women because though not contradicting religious convention, it implied serious criticism of women's status. Unfortunately, however, the book's hopeful

----

[3]Phelps [Ward], *Chapters from a Life* (Boston: Houghton, Mifflin Co., 1895), pp. 97-98.
[4]I follow the usage of historian Joan Kelly-Gadol, for whom "status" has an "expanded sense, to refer to woman's place and power -- that is, the roles and positions women hold in society by comparison to those of men." See "The Social Relation of the Sexes: Methodological Implications of Women's History," *Signs* 1 (Summer 1976): esp. 810.

Carol Farley Kessler

emphasis upon otherworldly rewards may have had the
dubious result of easing accommodation to an
unrewarding present.

Nonetheless, as historian Barbara Welter notes, if
"the equality of man before God expressed so
effectively in the Declaration of Independence had
little impact on women's lives . . . , the equality of
religious experience was something they could
personally experience, and no man could deny it to
them."[5] Coached by Winifred, the bereaved Mary Cabot
obtains such experience and records in a Journal her
mourning and growth toward self-dependence. With the
death in the Civil War of her brother Roy, Mary is
first overwhelmed by solitude, but with the arrival of
her widowed Aunt Winifred Forceythe, Mary begins to
overcome her despair. Through successive dialogues
with Winifred, each carefully recorded in her Journal,
Mary learns to live with her loss. Winifred offers not
the clergy's cold doctrine, but a consoling theology
adjusted to the needs of troubled human beings needing
relief from anguish. Sometimes her theology is
behavioral rather than verbal, as when she cradles Mary
in her lap as if a child. At other times, she urges
Mary to ignore the views of Deacon Quirk and the Rev.
Dr. Bland, that she pay lip service to the forms of
properly pious behavior. Winifred thus assumes her own
capacity to interpret the ways of God to women.

Winifred finds "God's great and glorious work" in
the immediate needs of those about her, painting for
Mary an earthly world where Roy's comforting spirit
still exists to console her and a heavenly home where
Mary will eventually join him. Foreshadowing the
utopian vision that Phelps would develop in *Beyond the
Gates* (1883), Winifred speaks of "new tastes and
capacities" that would be "enlarged" in one's heavenly
existence (p. 76). Contemporary clergy accusing Phelps
of "heresy . . . and atrocity," missed her point, which
was to create a system that could console women for
their loss, not only of those beloved, but of adequate
self-fulfillment as well.[6]

----

[5]Welter, p. 102.
[6]Bennett, pp. 50-52, discusses contemporary clerical
responses to *The Gates Ajar*; see also *McClure's Magazine*,
6 (May 1896): 515 and *Chapters*, pp. 118-119.

In addition to transmitting a view of Heaven as
compensation for earthly ills, Winifred gives others
life by encouraging each individual's self-dependence.
Acknowledging and responding supportively to others'
needs, she enhances their self-esteem. Mary's Journal
records her growth from a state of despondence over
losing the man upon whom she had relied to autonomy
without him. What Phelps advocates is behavior that
supports the development of others, rather than that
which exacts its own support from others.

Although Phelps developed her plan for *Beyond the
Gates* immediately after the publication of *The Gates
Ajar*, fifteen years elapsed before she actually wrote
it.[7] In the first *Gates* book, Phelps assures her
audience of reunion with loved relatives and depicts a
successful female ministry. In *Beyond the Gates* (1883)
she offers women the expectation of heavenly self-
fulfillment and reliable male support. Using the
convention of a dream vision, Phelps places forty-year-
old dying Mary into the arms of her deceased father.
Ill, then unconscious with brain fever, she envisions a
heavenly existence: her dead father has been
housekeeping alone, awaiting the arrival of his earthly
family, a reversal requiring a man to learn in Heaven
the life-maintaining activities left to women on earth.
Mary recounts that, though unmarried, she had not been
unhappy, but vigorously active in teaching, traveling,
nursing, and social work -- an inventory of acceptable
public activities for women. All of these occupations
concerned "more largely the experience of other people
than . . .[her] own" (p. 7). What she had missed, her
vision of Heaven reveals.

Phelps does not emphasize the economic or
technological wonders of a heavenly utopia, but rather
imagines a society that supports the self-realization
of its members. Since Mary had been facilitating
others' fulfillment, she must now learn to know her own
"whole nature" (p. 41) and follow its dictates. All of
her senses -- sight,touch, hearing -- are enhanced in
the new environment: she finds she has sensuous
capacities -- for example, to see music and hear color

----

[7]On plan, see Phelps to H. O. Houghton, 28 September
1883, Houghton Library, Harvard University; references
to *Beyond the Gates* appear parenthetically.

-- never before realized. Winifred of *The Gates Ajar*
(p. 76) had predicted such "enlarged capacities."
    Looking in upon her earthbound family, Mary sees
they appear deeply unhappy and possessed by great
unrest. She finds that, contrary to earthly existence,
in Heaven a woman can rest. Also, pleasure exists in
more intense and diverse modes than on earth: Mary
dares to be happy and finds this daring the very spirit
of her daily living. She must learn to risk, but gains
happiness from her resulting growth.
    As well as pleading for self-realization, *Beyond
the Gates* offers strong social criticism. From her
knowledge of mill town experience, Phelps includes, as
compensation for rampant deprivation, automatic access
to whatever residences, recreation, education, or
hospitalization citizens of a utopian city might
require to correct the earthly deficits with which they
arrive. Phelps objects to the effect of urban
industrialization upon human lives.
    The book closes, however, upon a more individual
note. Toward the end of the vision, after being joined
by her mother, Mary finds filial love inadequate for a
mature person. Meeting again a man whom she might have
loved twenty years ago, she rejoices in his "claiming"
her. However, upon waking from her dream, Mary says,
"Oh, Mother, I have Heaven in my heart at last" -- then
realizes that Heaven is no more (p.194). That Phelps
returns Mary to health and disappointment suggests the
emptiness of Mary's earlier claim that she was happy
though unmarried. In an 1882 letter to John Greenleaf
Whittier, written while composing the novel, Phelps
noted that she ought to have married when young in
order to have avoided later loneliness.[8]
    Perhaps the discrepancy between this ending and
Phelps's previous uncertainty about the benefits to a
woman of marriage can be explained by recalling that
her suitor had died just twenty years before, if we
assume the book was written the year before
publication. That death seems to have been symbolic to
her of lost possibility. In two years Phelps would
herself begin to move toward marriage. Perhaps in the
book's conclusion she begins to validate for herself

----

[8]Phelps to "My dear friend" [John Greenleaf Whittier],
14 May 1882, Alderman Library, University of Virginia.

such an alternative. But her fiction would never show a married woman happy.

Beyond the Gates, however, is less a personal testament than devastating social criticism. Precisely what is wished provides an index of what women missed and suggests why they flocked to read the *Gates* books. Phelps represented Heaven as offering to women what earth lacked -- namely, men whose socialization prepared them as adults to nurture the lives of women and children, and opportunities for women to experience pleasure, self-fulfillment, and the companionship of equals. For women particularly, "to be dead was to be alive to a sense of assured good chance that nothing in the universe could shake" (p. 72). Two other women would have concurred: Margaret Fuller (1810-1850), who wrote that she saw "no way out except through the gate of death" and novelist Kate Chopin (1851-1904), who in Edna Pontellier of *The Awakening* depicted a death preserving her from a dehumanizing and fragmented experience.[9] If we label these first two *Gates* books consolation literature, then we must understand the consolatory effect to include compensation not only for the death of loved ones, but as well, for deprivation in all the forms that women experienced.

In the third book of the series, *The Gates Between* (1887), Phelps made the central character not female but male, the physician Esmerald Thorne.[10] Her characterization of Esmerald reveals both her ideal and her critique of the male role. Having considered reunion with loved ones (1868) and provision of denied fulfillment and companionship (1883), Phelps turned her attention to the heavenly reform of an inconsiderate husband -- a theme so feminist that in Boston *The Woman's Journal,* edited by Lucy Stone, offered it as a subscription premium.[11] Phelps placed both fulfillment for women and reform of their male partners -- not surprisingly given nineteenth century practice -- in an otherworldly setting.

----

[9]Quoted by Barbara Cross, ed., *The Educated Woman in America* (New York: Teachers' College Press, 1965), pp. 29-30.
[10]References to *The Gates Between* appear parenthetically.
[11]*The Woman's Journal* 18 (October 1887): 32.

Carol Farley Kessler

        Using the device of a communication from the Other
Side, Phelps in Esmerald's narration depicts a man's
experience of heavenly reform.[12] Esmerald is catapulted
into Heaven from an accident caused by his runaway
horse. His enjoyment of his own power both allowed him
to drive a disastrously fast horse and also blinded him
to his other deficiencies. As Mary in Heaven discovers
her life unfulfilled, so Esmerald finds his life
underdeveloped. First of all he realizes that he has
had an unwholesome habit of classifying women as
"neuralgic, hysteric, dyspeptic" rather than as
"unselfish, intelligent, high-minded" (p. 5). Then he
perceives that as a boy, he was spoiled in being
trained to believe that only the male sex has the
liberty of free expression. By middle-age he had
trusted his power and charm to compensate for
irritability or uncontrolled anger. Hence, Esmerald's
healthy wife Helen had found that her former strength
dissolved as she learned to wait both for and upon her
husband. Phelps connects the love of power explicit in
Esmerald's behavior to ignorance of conditions
encouraging self-development in those close to him.
        Having discovered his shortcomings, Esmerald sets
upon a course of resocialization and domestication. No
longer able to control others, he must learn to wait
for their compliance. He finds his own humanity
narrowly trained to the intellectual: a patient's
capacity to love proves more lasting than his to
control. To learn the ways of loving nurture, Esmerald
receives the care of his now deceased son, about whose
former illness he had found his wife overly concerned.
He who loved fame, power, and love itself must perform
sundry invisible acts in support of his son's life --"

----

[12]For examples of authors familiar to Phelps who used
this device of other-worldly communication, see
Margaret Oliphant (1828-97), *A Little Pilgrim in the Unseen*
(1882); Harriet Prescott Spofford (1835-1921), "The
Amber Gods," *Atlantic* 5 (1860). Spofford's story
appears in Lee R. Edwards and Arlyn Diamond, eds.,
American Voices, American Women (New York: Avon Books,
1973), pp. 21-62. Phelps singled out this story as one
that had had a "subtle influence" upon the direction of
her own work ("Stories That Stay" *Century* 59, November
1910, p. 119).

lowly tasks [men] left . . . to women in the world below" (p. 185). Esmerald acknowledges his inadequacy as a parent: others have sight where he is blind. Once recognizing his deficiencies as husband, physician, and father, Esmerald can increase his vision. Where he had previously longed only to see Helen, he now desires to cultivate kindness in all earthly homes. He longs to increase human beings' sensitivity to the power of words -- of loving words to support, of cruel words to harm. Thus he becomes worthy of his wife's heavenly companionship. At last Helen "clung to [him] because she could not help it, and would not if she could" (p. 222).

Helen, merely a foil to Esmerald, is subordinated even in Heaven as she "crept" to him. Phelps, when focused upon a male character, seems less able to question such subordination than when she made a female central. Apparently the presence of masculinity so overwhelmed her that femininity automatically fell into its shadow even when her aim is equalizing the sexes. Characterization in both *Beyond the Gates* and *The Gates Between* shows that each sex could and must learn the strengths of the other because only thus might we fully experience our humanity. Where two gender roles had existed, Phelps demonstrates the efficacy of one -- that of realizing full human potential, regardless of sex.

In 1901 Phelps published her last *Gates* book, a dramatization and revision of her 1887 novel, using the same characters but now calling it *Within the Gates*. First serialized in *McClure's Magazine*, it was never staged.[13] In it, Phelps draws more sharply the lines

----

[13]*Within the Gates* (Boston, 1901); references appear parenthetically. The title repeats one used by Whittier for a memorial to Lydia Maria Child (1802-1880), "Within the Gate"; see Phelps's letter to Whittier, 8 March 1881, The Houghton Library, Harvard University. The play was first published in *McClure's Magazine*, 17 (May-July, 1901). For changed expectations of staging the play, see Phelps's letters to H. O. Houghton (23 November [1895], The Houghton Library, Harvard University) and to Elizabeth Garver Jordan (9 and 11 April 1900, Manuscripts and Archives Division, New York Public Library).

Carol Farley Kessler

contrasting the behavior of husband and wife so as to
emphasize the husband's error in being unsupportive.
Also, in several minor characters, she openly
criticizes the medical profession for vivisection
practices and for professional ethics that benefit
physicians, not patients. For example, to Dr. Carver's
ordering unnecessary surgery and Dr. Gazell's light-
hearted decision that a woman's irritability requires
operative cure, Phelps contrasts Dr. Thorne's diagnosis
for the patient's benefit and a nurse's sharp
observation that operative cure applied to "cross" men
could revolutionize society. Esmerald Thorne,
blameless in his professional ethics, thus appears the
more deficient in his marital and parental behavior.
As in the novel, Phelps reverses in Heaven the roles of
physician and patient, increasing the latter's status.
The most significant difference, however, is Phelps's
treatment of the reunion between Helen and Esmerald:
Helen, rather than creeping submissively toward her
husband, now stands tall, lifting Esmerald to her as he
begs forgiveness at her feet.
   We must surely see Phelps's *Gates* novels as
political actions. If the utopian novel is a means of
education for change, then *The Gates Between* is
precisely that, its concerns being implicit in earlier
Gates books. Here as in other concerns appearing in
her novels, Phelps was an innovator. As early as 1864,
she had begun to form in her mind the utopian
suggestions of *The Gates Ajar*. Writing her next two
Gates books in 1883 and 1887, she antedated Edward
Bellamy's 1888 *Looking Backward* and the proliferation of
utopian literature during the 1890's. She criticized
conventional assumptions about gender-specific child
care and housekeeping responsibilities left
unquestioned by most later utopian fiction of the
period 1888-1900.[14] In 1868 she demonstrated the
ineptitude of male as contrasted with female ministry.
In 1883, she showed a father keeping his heavenly home
while awaiting the return of his earthly family. In
1887, she put a husband to work caring for his young
son while awaiting his wife. The social criticism

----

[14]Kenneth M. Roemer, *The Obsolete Necessity: America in
Utopian Writings*, 1888-1900 (Kent State: Kent State
University Press, 1976), pp. 124-33.

implicit in Phelps's heavenly city paralleled her outspoken objections elsewhere to conditions she saw around her. In fact, British author and critic Margaret Oliphant (1828-1897), reviewing *The Gates Ajar* in *Blackwood's Magazine*, found it and Bret Harte's *The Luck of Roaring Camp* (1868) to be the first worthy American successors to the works of Hawthorne and Stowe.[15]

----

[15]*Blackwood's Magazine* 10 (October 1871): 422-42, quoted by H. S. Smith, Introduction, *The Gates Ajar*, p. xxiii, n. 22.

Much of this essay appears as part of chapter 2 in *Elizabeth Stuart Phelps*, TUSAS #434 (Boston: G.K. Hall, 1982). Dr. Evelyn Barish, chair of the "Nineteenth-Century American Women and Religion" section for NEMLA 1981, made helpful editorial suggestions for the version that was part of her panel.

WRIGHT'S *ISLANDIA:*
UTOPIA WITH PROBLEMS

Verlyn Flieger

In his introduction to Austin Tappan Wright's
Utopian novel, *Islandia*, Leonard Bacon comments that
Wright's imaginary world was "neither better nor worse
than things as they are. It was different, and thus
afforded a yardstick, a measure, a standard of
comparison."[1] This is a fair description. Unlike the
conventional ideal Utopian society, Wright's world is
populated with real people, facing real conflicts,
trying honestly and not always successfully to deal
with real problems. *Islandia* does not presume to solve
the dilemmas of the human race. But it does present a
realistic, alternative world with its own difficulties
and imperfections, one sufficiently different from our
own to offer a fresh perspective on the society in
which we live.
    Written in the early part of the twentieth
century, the book is decades ahead of its time in its
recognition of women as human beings rather than as
mere adjuncts to men. Wright has a surprising
awareness of what it is to be a woman in a man's world,
and a concomitant awareness of the problems attendant
on women's struggle for identity and fulfillment. He
wrote perceptively out of his own observations and
feelings that men and women could do better by one
another than they had so far. This is not to suggest
that he was a radical feminist. His vision is not an
extreme one, and is predicated on his perception of

----

[1]Bacon's comment, as well as all subsequent page
references to *Islandia*, pertain to the following
edition: Austin Tappan Wright, *Islandia* (New York:
Farrar and Rinehart, 1942).

clear differences between the sexes -- differences which define, but do not hamper roles. Still, his sympathy for women and his insight into their problems make him unusual not just in his own time, but in any time.

Let me tell you something of the setting and situation in the novel. The nation of Islandia is in the northern part of the Karain continent, somewhere in the southern hemisphere. The climate is temperate, the economy is agrarian, and the politics are conservative. The self-supportive family farm is the center of Islandian life and work, and the family is the most important social unit. The government is a parliamentary monarchy, lead by a king and run through a council of noblemen. The mode of life is pre-industrial, and the country is a stubborn anachronism in the modern world.

By contemporary standards, opportunities for women are limited. There are no careers open to them, for Islandia is not a career-oriented country. It is, in a sense, the last stronghold for the amateur; for the Islandian way is to pursue a skill or a talent, a craft or art for the love of it, not to become a professional, or to compete with others in the field. Nevertheless, Islandian women are free in a way that no woman of Wright's time was free unless she was a rebel against society. They are not only encouraged to be individuals, they are expected to be. When they marry they retain their own names. They have the sexual freedom to have love affairs without marriage, and while there may be personal or emotional consequences, there are no social ones. They are partners in marriage, not subservient to husbands. And while most Islandian women marry, there is no presure on them to do so or to suffer the tolerated half-life of the spinster. Above all, the Islandian woman, whether single or married, is expected to develop and nourish her own being, to have her own center and her own work.

While this sounds ideal in theory, Wright's exploration of the practice reveals as many problems in Islandia as there are in our own world. Not everyone fits the life equally well. Not everyone is equally happy with it. Wright's vision and his honesty are such that in Islandia, as here, there are no easy answers. Most problems are solved by compromise, and seldom to the complete satisfaction of all concerned. No world is perfect, but Islandia, recognizing that

there will always be problems, and leaving room to work
them out, manages as well as any, and better than most.
    The action of the book takes place in the years
from 1907 to 1910, and centers on the experience of
John Lang, assigned to Islandia as the first U.S.
Consul on the strength of his college friendship with
the young Islandian noble, Dorn. The narrative is in
the first person, and the point of view is always John
Lang's. The point of the book is the slow unfolding to
John of Islandian life and culture, and his growth
through the people he meets. What plot there is
concerns the question of opening hitherto isolationist
Islandia to foreign trade and development. The
conservatives, who are John's friends, want to preserve
the country as it is; the liberals want to catch up
with the rest of the world. John's very presence as
U.S. Consul is a threat to the Islandian way of life,
for it presages the incursion of U.S. interests and the
inevitable exploitation of the country.
    In the course of the book three women -- two
Islandians and one American -- affect John Lang's life,
and in so doing find their own lives affected and
changed, and their own qualities re-examined and re-
defined. The first is Dorna, sister of John's friend,
Dorn, and focus of all his romantic longings. She
warns John: "Do not wish to marry me" and so, of
course, he does. The second is Nattana, who is first
friend, then lover, and friend again. She accuses John
of having "pale pink emotions," and her words are a
direct sexual challenge. The last is Gladys, the
American, who brings to Islandia unconscious
assumptions about the role of women which make her
first weeks as an Islandian wife disturbingly, almost
frighteningly free.
    In each relationship, the meaning of the word
"love" is crucial, for where English has one word,
Islandian has three, with consequent narrowing and
sharpening of meaning. In his own mind and his own
language, John Lang "loves" both Dorna and Nattana.
They understand his feelings, and their own,
differently, for they use the Islandian words *ania* and
apia. John wants to marry Dorna; consequently, he
wants to sleep with her. This is *ania*, but only part
of *ania*, and she knows it, for it lacks the requisite
Islandian certainty of wanting to have her children,
and perpetuate her qualities through them. John wants
to sleep with Nattana, and therefore he is sure he

wants to marry her. This is *apia*, sexual desire,
honest and good in its kind, but, as she knows and he
doesn't, too limited an emotion to lead to successful
marriage. Both loves, as John experiences them, lack
the third and most important Islandian love, *alia*, love
of place and family. John's definitions, his
priorities, and hence his emotions, are confused and
confusing to him and to others. He has trouble in
sorting out his feelings, for as a foreigner, he has no
alia, and so has no framework in which to consider the
other two kinds of love.

If John is confused, the two Islandians are not.
But they are disturbed by his confusion and disturbed
by his presence in their country and their lives. Each
woman sees in John a possible escape from pressing
problems. Each tests herself with him, and against
him. Each, in her own way, grows beyond him, and in
using him to find herself, forces him to know himself
and his own nature better. The two together give him
an education in love, desire, and honesty, which make
him capable, finally, of knowing what love ought to be,
and finding it with and for Gladys. Dorna's concern is
whom to marry. Nattana's concern is whether to marry.
Gladys's concern is, having married, how to be together
with her husband by first finding and developing her
separateness from him.

Let us look first at Dorna. She is young (twenty-
three), beautiful, strong-willed, and ambitious. A
daughter of one of Islandia's most powerful and
influential families, great-niece of a former Premier,
she has a consuming interest in the politics of her
country, and an equally consuming fear of the foreign
development which may be imminent. For her, *alia* takes
precedence over any other love. She tries to explain
it to John: "I don't think anyone could understand who
has not lived on a place for hundreds of years as we
have. I feel our farm as a whole, as it is, as it was,
as it will be -- ours -- our land; and I feel ourselves
and its past and its future as one thing -- not me, not
us, but one thing by itself (I. p. 141). She tells
John of one of her ancestors, who sacrificed everything
he had to save his one child: "All the Dorns were in
that baby. . . . I was in that baby, John, and my
great-grandfather, who drove out the settlers, and the
Dorn who wasn't afraid of firearms although he had
never seen them before -- and my great-uncle, and my
brother . . . . He saved us all for hundreds of years.

The thing he wanted went on in the world (I. p. 328).
All of this is *alia*.
     What Dorna wants most is to remain single and have
her life and her being at the Dorn farm, the Island.
Her problem is that she has ambitions and desires which
she cannot fulfill alone. She wants to be instrumental
in shaping her country's future. Above all, she wants
to ward off foreign incursion, and to preserve
Islandia's slow-paced, simple way of life. Like any
Islandian woman, Dorna, if she marries, will have to
leave her *alia*, and try to form a new one with her "*alia*-
sharing lover," (Islandian has no word for wife or
husband). As a single woman she cannot be politically
effective, for the country is run by men. Married, she
can, but will have to give up part of herself.
     Two options offer themselves. One is to marry the
young king, Tor, and work with him on strengthening
Islandia's conservative policies and its independence
from the rest of the world. To do this she will have
to exchange her immediate *alia*, Dorn Island, which means
everything to her, for the larger *alia* of Islandia
itself. The other option is to marry John Lang. Since
he represents foreign interests, John's assimilation
into Islandian life would disarm the opposition, and
put John on the side of the conservatives. As a
homeless stranger, he would adopt Dorna's *alia* and thus
allow her to keep it for herself.
     Tor is Dorna's match in strength and certainty.
She says of him:

> I liked the power that is latent in him.
> I felt that he matched me . . . I saw
> myself helping him to use his powers. . .
> . I saw us founding a new line of Leaders
> . . . Somehow he was the man I wanted to
> live and work with, the only man who could
> ever satisfy one side of me. He seemed to
> give me scope to be myself. . . . Why was
> there a doubt in my mind? -- Can you
> understand a woman's wanting to marry a
> man because of his qualities and the life
> he offers her, and yet not wanting to be
> his wife? *Ania* but no real desire, only a
> sort of dread . . . (I. p. 666).

     What Dorna describes would be called, in our
terms, a marriage of convenience, one which satisfies

material and social needs, but leaves unfulfilled the romantic and sexual aspects of a relationship. But for an Islandian it is more, for it answers the need to find one's psychological match, and answers also the Islandian definition of *ania* as love which sees itself fulfilled in its descendents. But love in our sense of the word is missing; desire is missing; there seems to be no wholly satisfactory solution.

John Lang offers another possibility. He is a friend of her brother's, and seems to have an innate sympathy for the Islandian way of life which conflicts with his position as representative of a foreign government. Dorna is attracted to him, and very much aware of his "love" for her. But she knows he is using the English word, not Islandian *ania*. If she can find in him the match for her own powers, which she knows she must have, he may be an acceptable alternative to Tor and "*ania* but no real desire." And so she consciously leads him on, first offering and then withdrawing herself in a pattern of behavior confusing to John since he has no way of knowing whether it is only Dorna, or all Islandian women who behave thus. But she is not teasing him, she is testing him, exploring his strengths and weaknesses, hoping for his initiative, wanting to find in him a man as strong as she is.

Ultimately he fails the test. She is strongly attracted to John but she cannot feel *ania*, for he is not certain enough, not centered enough to match her. He has yet no clear idea of what he wants, or even of who he is. Marriage with him would be as much a marriage of convenience, albeit in different terms, as marriage with Tor. She tells him:

> I would make you unhappy. I would not be happy myself, for I would always remember my lost chances. I would have married you because I loved my home most. . . . But I wanted you, John -- I wanted you then to be my man. . . . And all the time I was on the thinnest of thin ice, hoping it would break, hoping you would take charge of yourself and me! (I. p. 704).

Neither man is all of what she wants. Whichever option Dorna chooses, she will be forced to give up part of herself and part of her life. Her experience

with John forces her to understand that she needs
someone strong enough to help her realize her ambitions
for her country. In the end she chooses Tor and the
larger stage of political life. As queen she is a
member of the king's Council, and has a voice in
governmental affairs. At the crucial Council meeting
to decide the question of foreign trade she speaks
passionately against it, and helps to sway the vote in
favor of Islandian isolation and independence. In
making her decision she has taken charge of her own
life and her family's future. But she does not deceive
herself about what she has given up, or about the
nature of her marriage. It is a compromise, and in
some important ways unfulfilling. She knows what is
missing, and with characteristic Islandian clear-
headedness and honesty she acknowledges it to John at
their final meeting.

     She arranges an interview with John to have, as
she calls it, a full reckoning, to explain herself to
him, to tell him why she has done as she has. She
wants to put their relationship in the proper
perspective, so that there will be no half-hopes, no
lingering doubts or unresolved tensions, no regrets.
She sets him free, and by doing so, shows him that he
is strong enough to accept that freedom. He has grown,
and learned to recognize a lost good, to take the good
from it and let the rest go, and to use the strength
gained in the experience to build a future. In short,
to be Islandian, not American.

     Nattana, John's next love, is in a more difficult
position than Dorna, for she is not happy with her
family, and has no certain place to go if she leaves
them. She is a few years younger than Dorna, and unlike
Dorna, she has a craft. She is a weaver and a tailor,
but as one of her brothers remarks, it is a craft which
requires other people to make it grow. Her family is
large, full of conflicts, and remarkably un-Utopian.
Within it Nattana finds no scope to be herself. Her
father, a stubborn and opinionated autocrat, has
violated the Islandian custom of limiting the size of
families. He does not believe in birth control, has
married twice, and produced eight children, far too
many to be supported by the two rather meager family
farms. "If we girls marry," says Nattana, "that is one
thing, but if we don't . . . we will be very crowded"
(I. p. 452). And crowded is an unusual condition in
spacious Islandia.

Nattana is not at all sure she wants to marry. She has seen her father force her younger sister, Nettera, into a loveless marriage because she became pregnant. Nattana feels strongly that Nettera should have been allowed to remain single, have her baby and follow music, her one pursuit. But her father, trying to reduce the congestion in the family, has seen a way to get rid of one daughter and a future grandchild. He acts without consideration for his children's Islandian right to be free to be themselves.

Nattana is a misfit, banished from the Lower Farm because of her disagreements with her father, and feeling unwanted at the Upper Farm, where her older sister and two of her brothers are working to make themselves a new *alia*. She has her weaving, but no market for it in her new surroundings. John Lang, lonely, sensitive, and out-of-place himself, seems to offer a way out, and she questions him closely about life in the United States, how women live, what they do, what they wear, whether they marry or remain single, and how they live their lives. She is clearly comparing it not just to life in Islandia, but to *her* life in Islandia. As might be expected, life in the United States comes out a poor second -- no *alia*, a cramped house and only a housewife's duties, her craft of weaver and tailor denigrated to seamstress, her individuality subsumed in her husband's life and his profession. She cannot imagine what John's life there is really like, nor can she imagine what her life as his wife would be.

Nevertheless, John and Nattana, each for separate reasons unhappy and out of place, draw closer and closer together. The surface of their relationship is easy friendship, but both are increasingly aware of a growing sexual attraction which colors their moments together and is the unspoken undertone to all their conversations. John, already off-balance from his unsuccessful pursuit of Dorna, does not know how to handle the situation, or how to proceed from where they are. It is Nattana who forces ackowledgement of their feelings in a little dialogue which shows clearly how far ahead of John she is in her perception and her honesty:

'Shall we face it?' she demanded.
'Face what?'
'What we feel now.'

-103-

VERLYN FLIEGER

      'Yes, Nattana.'
      'What do you feel, Johnlang?'. . .
how could I say it in Islandian where
there were so few muffling words?
      'I feel at least *apiata*,' I said.
Blood flamed in my face and it suddenly
seemed that I had uttered a brutal,
indecent thing.
      'So do I!' she declared. . .
.'There!' she continued. 'That is said!
And *apiata* either dies or becomes something
else, Johnlang' (I. p. 547).

    John's difficulty is obvious. He is having to
call a spade a spade. He cannot say he feels love, for
Islandian has no such "muffling words." He cannot call
it *ania*, for that more nearly describes his feeling for
Dorna. *Apia* is all that is left. The Islandian
language forces him to be honest with Nattana and
himself.
    As their affair progresses, he dodges the reality
of the situation by insisting over and over that
Nattana marry him, without any clear idea of what that
marriage will be, or even of where it will be. Their
sexual rapport is at first complete in their identical
passion and mutual need. But their passion is not
mutual, nor their need identical, and as time goes on
each realizes (Nattana first), that *apia*, as an end in
itself, is bound to die.
    Nattana is the first to let go. Having tried
physical love knowing it is not *ania*, knowing her
feeling for John will go no further nor will his for
her, she makes the break. He is as aware of the
unfruitfulness of their situation as she is, but less
willing to face it, and he presses her to explain:

      'Tell me! Is there someone else?'
      'No!' she cried in fury. 'There is no
one else, and there is not likely to be,
for I know myself better. I am not what I
thought I was; and I don't want men to
come too close. I want other things -- to
be at home, to work. Through you I have
had my glimpse at marriage and *ania*. I am
going home to make everything up with my
father -- and to live single hereafter.'
      'Have I ruined marriage for you

Nattana? If so --'
          'Ruined it? Of course not! But my
eyes have been opened. I like the thought
of being single and restrained -- and of
working hard. . . . I want no second best
things with men.'
          'Was what we had second best?'
          'Of course it was, or we would be
married now. . . . Our liking for each
other is not second best. Don't confuse
the two things, Johnlang' (I. pp.
744-45).

          The key to Nattana's development is her statement:
"I am not what I thought I was." Her experience with
John Lang has been a voyage of self-discovery greater
than that of Dorna. Dorna has known herself, and
needed only to discover which facets of her nature were
most important. Nattana has come to know herself, and
although it is not the self she expected, she is
content. Beyond this, she is able to distinguish
between the "second best" of her *apia* and the honest
friendship which now exists between her and John. This
is as close to a perfectly satisfactory solution as
Wright comes, and it is predicated on the room to move
about which Islandian culture grants the individual.
Only in Islandia would Nattana have been free to try
out a love which she thought she wanted but which she
knew instinctively was limited. Only in Islandia could
she have been free enough to acknowledge that it did
not work, and strong enough to let it go with no
lingering and no regrets. Only in Islandia could she
have tried out a kind of love and learned from it with
no bitter aftermath, no social or psychological
repercussions.
          Her decision is made for her own benefit, but it
is right for John Lang as well. Having graduated, so
to speak, from both Dorna and Nattana, John returns to
the United States for a trial year during which he must
decide if he wants to make Islandia his permanent home.
In Boston he renews his friendship with Gladys Hunter,
a girl of seventeen when he left, and now a young woman
of twenty. Through a year's slow courtship, John
unfolds Islandia and its ways to Gladys, who alone of
his countrymen seems to understand and appreciate what
he has found there. He comes to love her, and has
learned from his experiences with Dorna and Nattana to

be able to evaluate that love and know it for a true one, for *ania*, needing only *alia* to give it permanence.

John returns to Islandia and to the farm which his friendship with Dorn has enabled him to purchase. A cable from shipboard carries his proposal of marriage to Gladys, and she accepts and comes out to join him. But this is not the end of the story. As a bride, Gladys has much to learn about her new situation, but even more to unlearn. She comes to Islandia full of love and hope, ready to assimilate herself into its life and ways, only to find that she is bound by social and cultural expectations so deeply ingrained that she did not know they were there.

Gladys's unconscious assumption is that her life will be contained in that of her husband, that she will take her identity from him and find her fulfillment in his work and her support of that work. She will be, in short, a housewife. Her first months in Islandia are months of unmet expectations, of confusion when she finds that John does not expect or want her to be dependent on him, and of a surprising emptiness when she tries to forge her own place and her own identity. All her actions at first are motivated by what she thinks John wants, and to find that he wants her to satisfy first her own needs and to want what she wants, leaves her at a loss. The first months of their marriage are strained, and John and Gladys are truly together only in their moments of lovemaking. What any Islandian woman has from birth, Gladys must create for herself -- her separate identity, her own center, her knowledge of what is good for her, not for John.

Wright's view of women is nowhere more sympathetic than in his portrayal of Gladys, not ambitious like Dorna, not rebellious like Nattana but a woman whose potential she herself is unaware of, and reluctant to explore. It seems clear that in finding her feet in Islandia, Wright's Gladys becomes the paradigm of what he felt women could and should be -- fully developed human beings, strong in themselves, comfortable and secure in the knowledge of who they are, and out of that security able to give without any fear of giving up. Wright's solution to Gladys's problem of how to be Islandian is one which today's feminists might deplore, for it is her decision, independent of John's wishes, to become pregnant. But in the context of Wright's Utopia, it is both an individual gesture and a commitment to a way of life, for the significance of

the action is that Gladys thinks well enough of herself
and her qualities to want to perpetuate them, to give
to Islandia something it did not have before, and to be
with John the founder of an *alia* for generations yet
unborn.

No utopian model can ever be fully realized in the
real world, but the closer one comes to that real world
the more likely it may be to have something of value to
offer. The nature of Islandia and the realness of its
problems make it an attainable, imitable, and
persuasive alternate world.

URSULA LE GUIN'S
THE LEFT HAND OF DARKNESS:
ANDROGYNY AND THE FEMINIST UTOPIA

Jewell Parker Rhodes

In "*Is Gender Necessary?*" Ursula Le Guin argues
that *The Left Hand of Darkness* is, in part, a feminist
thought-experiment whereby Gethenians as androgynes
become a heuristic for determining essential humanity
without lifelong cultural conditioning of gender roles.
In other words, "[she] eliminated gender to find out
what was left."[1]
The novel's female Ekumenical investigator notes:

> When you meet a Gethenian you cannot and
> must not do what a bisexual naturally
> does, which is to cast him in the role of
> Man or Woman, while adopting towards him a
> corresponding role dependent on your
> expectations of the patterned or possible
> interactions between persons of the
> opposite sex. Our entire pattern of
> socio-sexual interaction is non-existent
> here. They cannot play the game. They do
> not see one another as men or women. This
> is almost impossible for our imagination
> to accept. What is the first question we
> ask about a newborn baby?
> Yet you cannot think of a Gethenian
> as 'it.'

----

[1]Ursula Le Guin, "Is Gender Necessary?" *The Language of
the Night*, ed. Susan Wood (New York: G.P. Putnam's Sons,
1979), p. 163.

> One is respected and judged only as a human being. It is an appalling experience.[2]

While the lack of sex roles may be an appalling experience for a future bisexual race, it is perhaps more appalling for feminists (futuristic or otherwise) that androgyny as a heuristic for uncovering "essential humanity" is itself flawed by historic patriarchical biases. Unfortunately, few feminists -- including Le Guin -- recognize this point. Indeed Virginia Woolf, Simone de Beauvoir, and psychologist Sandra L. Bem have all affirmed androgyny as a pre-requisite for women's liberation. Carolyn Heilbrun, in her now classic *Toward A Recognition of Androgyny*, concurs:

> . . . our future salvation lies in a movement away from sexual polarization and the prison of gender toward a world in which individual roles and modes of behavior can be freely chosen. The ideal toward which I believe we should move is best described by the term 'androgyny.' This ancient Greek word -- from *andro* (male) and *gyn* (female) -- defines a condition under which characteristics of the sexes . . . are not rigidly assigned. Androgyny seeks to liberate the individual from the confines of the appropriate.[3]

It seems irrational not to prefer the implied idealistic vision of human development and interaction embodied in Heilbrun's definition. However, it is my argument that androgyny as a possible utopian device aimed at exploding our culture's sexual restraints is a deception. The myth inherently reinforces and encourages the stereotyping feminists would so dearly love to deny.

----

[2]Ursula Le Guin, *The Left Hand of Darkness* (New York: Ace Books, 1969; rpt. 1980), pp. 94-95. Further references will be followed by LHD and page number.
[3]Carolyn G. Heilbrun, *Toward A Recognition of Androgyny* (New York: Alfred A. Knopf, 1973), pp. ix-x.

Jewell Parker Rhodes

* * *

The androgyne ranks as one of humankind's oldest
archetypes. Both Eastern and Western cosmogonies posit
that at creation, there was the androgyne -- a
primordial unity of sexually undifferentiated
entities.[4] Consequently, the splitting of the androgyne
"mark[ed] the end of mythic time and the beginning of
[social] reality"[5] as we know it.

In Plato's *Symposium*, Aristophanes states
androgynes were "complete spheres" whose shape was
symbolic of their perfect nature. When they aspired to
be as gods, they were cut in half, divided into men and
women and thus, debilitated.[6] Norman O. Brown points
out that "cabalistic mysticism has interpreted Genesis
1:27 -- 'God created man in his own image . . . male
and female he created them' -- as implying the
androgynous nature of God and human perfection before
the Fall."[7] Both Brown and Plato parallel each other's
argument that the first humans, desiring that they may
eat from the Tree of Knowledge, brought about the fall
of the androgyne; they associated humankind's original
sin with the division of sexual roles.[8] Jung later
popularized the notion that since androgyny is a
biological impossibility, mythic fusion could be
psychologically regained by tapping the unconscious
mind. Jung defines the unconscious mind as "the
opposite gender from the conscious mind: the

----

[4]N.B. Hayles, "Androgyny, Ambivalence, and
Assimilation," *Ursula K. Le Guin: Writers of the 21st
Century Series*, ed. Joseph D. Olander and Martin Harry
Greenberg (New York: Taplinger Publishing, 1979), p.
98.
[5]Ibid.
[6]*The Symposium of Plato*, trans. S. Gordon (Mass.:
University of Mass. Press, 1970), pp. 61-68.
[7]Norman O. Brown, *Life Against Death: The Psychoanalytic
Meaning of History* (1950; rpt. New York: Random House,
Modern Library Paperback, n.d.), pp. 133-34.
[8]A similar version of this history of the androgyne
appears in my article, "Female Stereotypes in Medieval
Literature: Androgyny and the Wife of Bath," *Journal of
Women's Studies in Literature*, 1, No. 4 (Autumn 1979), p.
351.

unconscious for a man is his *anima* (from the feminine form of the Greek word for spirit); for a woman, it is her *animus* (the corresponding masculine form)."[9]

All the myth's retellings encompass the promise of a totality of human expression and behavior; the unity of the androgyne is presumably awesome. However, while such versions of the myth seem to negate male/female polarizations, they do so by seducing us to believe that a man alone, a woman alone, is imperfect. As a result, romantics throughout history have accepted the androgyny myth as justification for heterosexual unions -- "marriage" via sexual intercourse and by legal contract.[10] Feminists evading the romantics' anti-homosexuality notions,[11] have favored Jung's "psychological androgyne," the unearthing of latent characteristics from within -- the masturbatory fusion of self with self, female consciousness with male unconsciousness. This feminist interpretation nonetheless conveys in a more subtle form the romantic view that a woman is in and of herself is lacking; she needs maleness (though, of course, transposed to a spiritual, inanimate level) to be complete.

Yet isn't it perhaps more appropriately feminist and more realistic to suggest that one of the pre-conditions for utopian society is the belief that men and women, excluding physical differences, are equal? Men and women are not deficient, as androgyny implies, in their capacity for human response; rather, social conditioning modifies and restricts behavior to gender categories. By adopting even a psychologically androgynous model, feminists reinforce and internalize society's otherwise external gender-based categories: "maleness is in me," a woman now says; "my *animus* reborn." But can we define "male" and "female" without resorting to distinctions influenced by social and patriarchal programming? Rationality is male; emotion, female: "simply from a linguistic point of view, the

----

[9]Hayles, p. 99.
[10]Cynthia Secor, "Androgyny: An Early Reappraisal," *Women's Studies*, vol. 2, No. 2 (1974), pp. 167-168.
[11]For more detailed analysis of the androgyne and the homosexual, see Catharine R. Stimpson, "The Androgyne and the Homosexual," *Women's Studies*, vol. 2, No. 2 (1974).

myth   is   self-defeating.   Politically   the   myth   is
subversive. . . ."[12]
  For the myth to be non-subversive, we would have
to conjure the impossible and enter "pre-mythic" time
during which androgynes existed possibly as sensory,
visual archetypes unhampered by the social construct of
language. We would have to discover the psychological
and spiritual significance of the androgyne unnamed,
stripped of sexist denotative and connotative meanings.
Only   in   "pre-mythic"   time   could   we   perhaps   draw
sustenance from a vision which psychically allows for
and encourages an infinite range of human attitudes and
actions.
  Overlooking   linguistic   difficulties,   feminists
might argue that since men and women are depicted as
equals, androgyny remains a liberating force; or, more
accurately, men and women are depicted as being equally
unequal to the mythic state. A man without development
of   his   *anima*   is   less   than   the   perfectly   fused
androgyne. A woman without development of her *animus* is
similarly flawed.   In the search for their respective
lost halves of identity, neither a man nor a woman has
an   advantage   by   virtue   of   their   sex.   "Essential
humanity," feminists maintain, lies in the completion
of self -- the filling of the void for both sexes. One
cannot help but wonder if men and women, then, are
analogous to four ounces of water in an eight ounce
glass. Are we half-empty or half-full?
  However   Barbara   Gelphi   in   "The   Politics   of
Androgyny" notes, while "there are two possible sorts
of   androgynes: the   masculine   personality . . .
completed   by   the   feminine   and   the   feminine . . .
completed by the masculine," versions of the myth have
historically emphasized the male completion model.[13]
"In fact, [male completion] theories . . . simply take
for granted a woman's inferiority: it is impossible for
the female . . . to contain masculine intelligence and
spirituality, while it is not only possible but natural
for the [male] to be filled and fulfilled by feminine

----

[12]Daniel   A.   Harris,   "Androgyny: The   Sexist   Myth   in
Disguise," *Women's Studies*, vol 2, no. 2 (1974), p. 151.
[13]Barbara   Charlesworth   Gelphi,   "The   Politics   of
Androgyny," *Women's Studies*, vol. 2, no.2 (1974), p.
151.

emotion and physicality."[14]

For example, Jung felt women ought to repress their *animus* "in order to protect men from loss of ego, pride, economic power, and sexual security."[15] He argued:

> It fits in with [a woman's] nature to keep her ego and her will in the background, so as not to hinder the man in any way, and to invite him to realize his intentions with regard to her person.[16]

> . . . no one can get round the fact that by taking up a masculine profession, studying and working like a man, woman is doing something not wholly in accord with, if not directly injurious to, her feminine nature.[17]

By discouraging the female completion model, Jung reveals his sexism; he "reveals [too] with utmost clarity how insidiously the myth can be manipulated to maintain male dominance."[18]

Feminists' desire to adopt androgyny as a goal for human development and interaction suggests a destructive irony -- destructive and ironic because the myth represses women while offering a glimmer of utopian self-completion. Androgyny as interpreted by our culture, "is at heart a reactionary and discriminatory concept;"[19] it swallows us in the same sexist categories we meant to escape.

* * *

----

[14] Ibid., pp. 151-152.
[15] Harris, p. 180.
[16] C.G. Jung, "Women In Europe," *Civilization in Transition*, trans. R.F.C. Hull (New York: Pantheon Books, 1964). Quoted by Harris, p. 180.
[17] Ibid.
[18] Harris, pp. 180-181.
[19] Carol Brown, "The Lure of Androgyny in the Case for a Female Aesthetic in Fiction," (unpublished paper), p. 14.

Jewell Parker Rhodes

While Le Guin denies that *The Left Hand of Darkness* is utopian fiction -- and rightly so as witnessed by the novel's conclusion -- there seems little doubt that androgyny holds utopian promise for her, since, on Gethen:

> . . . Anyone can turn his hand to anything. This sounds very simple, but its psychological effects are incalculable. The fact that everyone between seventeen and thirty-five or so is liable to be . . . 'tied to childbearing,' implies that no one is quite so thoroughly 'tied down' here as women, elsewhere, are likely to be -- psychologically or physically. Burden and privilege are shared . . . equally . . . . Consider: There is no division of humanity into strong and weak halves, protective/protected, dominant/submissive, owner/chattel, active/passive (LHD. pp. 93-94).

Le Guin's biological androgynes, presumably free from sexual stereotyping, have helped to produce a world without war, without rape, and without technological exploitation. This pleasant state exists, states Le Guin, because the "'female principle' is basically anarchic. It values order without constraint, rule by custom not by force. It has been the male who enforces and breaks laws. On Gethen, these two principles are in balance: the decentralizing against the centralizing, the flexible against the rigid, the circular against the linear."[20]

Regrettably, Le Guin's explanation for Gethen's "utopian-like" conditions reinforces the fact that language inserts sexist connotations into a myth supposedly devoid of discrimination. Do we truly know that women are "decentralizing," "flexible," and "circular?" Clearly, for Le Guin, these words connote meaning in reference to women; but such connotations are distinct from whether or not the words *define*

----

[20] Le Guin, "Is Gender Necessary?," p. 165.

femaleness. Isn't it social conditioning which causes us to accept men as opposites of women -- "centralizing," "rigid," and "linear?" Again, in the interest of feminism, it seems more productive to assert that all behavioral terms (excluding physiological distinctions) which refer to men are equally applicable to women. A woman can be "decentralizing" or "centralizing," "rigid" or "flexible" depending upon the circumstances of a given situation. Neither a woman nor a man, however, is predisposed to act out one set of "gender-based" categories over another.

Le Guin is well aware that language occasionally obstructs truth. The Ekumenical investigator reports her "very use of the pronoun [he]. . . leads me continually to forget that the Karhider I am with is not a man, but a manwoman" (LHD. p. 95). Yet, when writing the novel, Le Guin "refus[ed] to mangle English by inventing a pronoun for 'he/she.' 'He' is the generic pronoun, damn it. . . ."[21]

While Le Guin is not to be faulted for her grammar, one must consider whether as an artist her obligation is to grammar or to producing more valid results from her fictional thought-experiment. If as an artist she can invent a new futuristic world with new religions and new cultural groupings, then, can't she invent new words to depict accurately her vision of the androgyne? Perhaps this argument is extreme: but Le Guin's fictional world is called *Gethen*, Gethen's religions are called *Handdara* and *Yomesh*, and the planet's cultural groups are named *Karhiders* and *Orgota*; given these nouns are alien to English, would it not be equally simple to refer to the Gethenians in such a way as to reflect better their ambisexual being? A pronoun by any other name?. . . .

"Truth," writes Le Guin, "is a matter of the imagination" (LHD. p. 1). If so, would the invention of a new pronoun deflect interest from the novel's plot and characterization? Or, would a new pronoun enhance the novel by forcing readers "to see" and "to think" of the characters as they really are -- alien in their androgyny? Does the pronoun "he" in reference to the androgynenot insist upon a vision of maleness which is

----

[21] Ibid., p. 168.

inaccurate to the text?[22] Only Genly Ai is entitled to
the pronoun "he"; consequently, he, like the readers,
"see[s] and judge[s] as an alien. . ." (LHD. p. 5).
Pronoun distinctions between Ai and the Gethenians
would make more immediate the xenophobia which must be
overcome. A human and androgyne are not one and the
same; language should make the differences clear.

Gethenians are, in truth, biological androgynes
only five-sixths of the time:

> The sexual cycle averages 26 to 28 days .
> . . .For 21 or 22 days the individual is
> *somer*, sexually inactive, latent. . . .
> on the 22nd or 23rd day the individual
> enters *kemmer*, estrus. In this first
> phase of kemmer . . . he remains
> completely androgynous. Gender, and
> potency, are not attained in isolation. A
> Gethenian in first-phase kemmer, if kept
> alone or with others not in kemmer,
> remains incapable of coitus. . . . When
> the individual finds a partner in kemmer,
> hormonal secretion is further stimulated .
> . . until in one partner either a male or
> female hormonal dominance is established.
> The genitals engorge or shrink
> accordingly, foreplay intensifies, and the
> partner, triggered by the changes, takes
> on the other sexual role . . . (LHD. p.
> 90).

Second phase kemmer, which divides Gethenians' sexual
characteristics, is necessary for reproduction. It
should be noted, however, that the sexual union of
"kemmering" Gethenians is a variation of the romantic
theme of androgyny; heterosexual sex restores
primordial unity. "To vow kemmering" approximates
fidelity in marriage. Consequently, it seems suspicious
and contradictory for an androgyne, via temporary
separation of the sexes, to retreat from "his/her"

----

[22]Among those who have raised the problem of the
generic pronoun, see Pamela J. Annas, "New Worlds, New
Words: Androgyny in Feminist Science Fiction," *Science
Fiction Studies*, vol. 5 (1978), p. 151.

independent unity to be *dependent* on the sexual role adoption of another. Why should a "miraculous male" androgyne suddenly need a "female" (and the converse) for sexual intercourse? It appears Le Guin could not conceive of Gethenian sexuality without first relegating her characters to male/female sexual roles. Perhaps, as in the matter of language, Le Guin's imagination was limited by her own cultural conditioning. Perhaps there lies a terror in androgynes being complete unto themselves or in the notion of an "independent unity" sexually joining with a similar unified, independent being.

Despite the emphasis on heterosexuality, some feminists view Gethenian biology as a psychic metaphor for the journey towards human liberation. Is it possible, though, to make the leap from biology to metaphor when characterization suggests androgynes -- discounting when they are "males" and "females" engaged in sex -- are not men/women but merely men? According to Le Guin:

> The pronouns wouldn't matter . . . if I had been cleverer at *showing* the 'female' component in *action*. Unfortunately, the plot and structure that arose . . . cast the Gethenian protagonist, Estraven, almost exclusively into roles which we are culturally conditioned to perceive as 'male'-- a prime minister, . . .a political schemer, a fugitive, a prison-breaker, a sledge-hauler. . . .[23]

Again, the irony of androgyny is that social conditioning prevents us from seeing "utopian fusion" without first assigning gender-based roles. In one sense, Le Guin's artistic task to characterize men/women was impossible without her being influenced by our culture's susceptibility to sexist stereotyping. Le Guin admits she "left out too much. One does not see Estraven . . . in any role which we automatically perceive as 'female': and therefore, we tend to see him as a man. This is the real flaw in the book. . . ."[24]

----

[23]Le Guin, "Is Gender Necessary?," p. 168.
[24]Ibid.

Jewell Parker Rhodes

Unfortunately, androgyny as a heuristic for exploring the essence of humanity cannot do so without reflecting pervasive biases. Patriarchy and misogyny color the writing of even so ardent a feminist as Le Guin: Genly makes several damaging references about the femaleness of androgynes throughout the novel. At one point, he refers to the "effeminate deviousness" in their behavior (LHD. p. 14); at other points, he comments:

> . . . at the table Estraven's performance had been womanly, all charm and tact and lack of substance, specious and adroit (LHD. p. 12).

> . . . I thought of him as my landlady, for he had fat buttocks that wagged as he walked, and a soft fat face, and a prying, spying, ignoble, kindly nature (LHD. p. 48).

> . . . but they did not go to war. They lacked it seemed the capacity to *mobilize*. They behaved like animals, in that respect; or like women (LHD. pp. 48-49).

> They tended to be stolid, slovenly, heavy, and to my eyes effeminate -- not in the sense of delicacy, etc., but in just the opposite sense; a gross, bland fleshiness, a bovinity without point or edge (LHD. p. 176).

While the preceding comments might reflect Genly's sexism rather than Le Guin's, they nonetheless seem unnecessarily damaging portraits which reinforce our culture's negative perceptions of women. But Le Guin would have us believe that during the trek across the ice, Genly grows dramatically in his understanding and acceptance of the androgyne. He overcomes his distrust of the man/woman Estraven. Or, most notably, he overcomes his distrust of the woman in Estraven: a "sudden assurance of friendship between us rose: a friendship so much needed . . . that it might as well be called, now as later, love" (LHD. p. 248). Ai can even contemplate -- without distaste -- having sexual intercourse with the androgyne. He learns to see

-118-

Gethenians with "not a man's face and not a woman's, [but with] a human face, [this was] a relief to me, familiar, right" (LHD. p. 296).

However, despite Genly's growth, he cannot help but remark about the now dead Estaven's son: "(he had a girl's quick delicacy in his looks and movements, but no girl could keep so grim a silence as he did) . . ." (LHD. p. 299). This sexist comment undermines the notion of Genly's growth and liberation from gender distinctions. It might be meant to reflect that Genly remains alien and can only temporarily escape his social conditioning; this interpretation, however, seems seriously at odds with Le Guin's thematic intention. Or, possibly, the comment reflects how insidious sexism can be -- even for a feminist author. The novel ends with the *androgyne* child exclaiming: "Will you tell us how *he* [Estraven] died? -- Will you tell us about the other worlds out among the stars -- the other kinds of *men*, the other lives?" (LHD. p. 301; italics mine).

Before concluding "Is Gender Necessary?," Le Guin claims:

> It seems to be men, more often than women, who thus complete my work for me: I think because men are often more willing to identify as they read with poor, confused, defensive Genly, the Earthman, and therefore to participate in his painful and gradual discovery of love.[25]

Yet I suggest that men more often than women "complete" *The Left Hand of Darkness* because Le Guin's own social conditioning skews the tale until a preference for the male viewpoint is established.[26] Like other historic retellings of the myth, the male completion model of the androgyne is favored and dominant.

----

[25] Ibid.
[26] For examples of how men and women might "complete" *The Left Hand of Darkness*, see the articles by Norman N. Holland and Marleen Barr in *Future Females: A Critical Anthology*, ed. Marleen Barr (Bowling Green: Popular Press, 1981).

Jewell Parker Rhodes

There is no question that Le Guin is an excellent
and imaginative writer. But, unfortunately, the
androgyny theme is too complex, too interwoven with our
culture's misconceptions for it to succeed as a
"feminist thought experiment."

* * *

There is a third completion model where men and
women as psychic androgynes exist as equals and join
together by mutual choice -- not to correct
deficiencies; not to imply that they are not sufficient
unto themselves. They fuse for the realistic, rather
than romantic, expectation of human sharing. *This* is
the power of the androgyne. Such a utopian ideal might
exist in a future even beyond that of the Gethenians.
When future writers live in a world which is free from
sexual stereotyping, then the spirit of the androgyne
will have the chance to be captured in words. But
perhaps by then the task will seem gratuitous.

TRUTH AND ART IN WOMEN'S WORLDS:
DORIS LESSING'S *MARRIAGES BETWEEN*
ZONES THREE, FOUR, AND FIVE

Lee Cullen Khanna

And you her creatures, whom she workes upon,
And have your last, and best concoction
From her example, and her vertue, if you
In reverence to her, do thinke it due,
That no one her praises thus rehearse,
As matter fit for Chronicle, not verse;
Vouchsafe to call to minde that God did make
At last, and lasting'st peece, a song. He spake
To Moses to deliver unto all
That song, because hee knew they would let fall
The Law, the Prophets, and the History,
But keepe the song still in their memory.

                    John Donne
            "An Anatomie of the World"

     Song, whether as music, story, poem, painting or
other type of art, is valued as highly in the utopian
worlds created by women as it was by John Donne in his
tribute to the archetype of female wisdom.[1] In fact,

----

[1]John Donne's two long poems, "An Anatomie of the
World," and "The Progresse of the Soul," (better known
as the "Anniversaries") both lament the death of
Elizabeth Drury, daughter of Donne's patron. Yet the
ostensible death of a young girl simply provides the
occasion for Donne's profound meditation on the world's
loss of devotion, wisdom, integrity -- qualities he

Lee Cullen Khanna

the several utopian novels written by women in the last
decade include substantial consideration of aesthetic
pleasure or creativity.[2] In *Woman on the Edge of Time*,
for example, Marge Piercy focuses attention on the
artistic "events" that occupy a central place in her
utopia, Mattopoisett. These communal occasions use
song, dance, drama, poetry, elaborate costumes, and
even holograms, and they demonstrate the society's
deliberate cultivation of aesthetic awareness.

The high estimation of art in feminist utopian
fiction, however, distinguishes that fiction from the
tradition of utopian speculation. Plato certainly
considers artists in his classical utopian work, the
Republic, but approves only of artists who are
subservient to the philosophic precepts of the state.
Since art, in Plato's view, appeals simply to the
emotions, it is far removed from truth. Thus, the
rational guardians must control artists so that they
imitate only those actions that the state deems
beautiful and good.[3] Of course, Plato recognizes the
power of art and pays more attention to it than most
subsequent utopists. In Thomas More's *Utopia*, little
mention is made of art at all. Although music and
incense may accompany utopian citizens during their

----

seems, in these poems, to associate with the archetypal
feminine. Although the "shee" in the poems has been
variously identified by scholars, the editor of the
standard text, Frank Manley, seems closest to the
spirit of the poems when he suggests that some ancient
idea of female wisdom, Astraea or Sapientia, is
probably intended. See Frank Manley, ed., John Donne:
The Anniversaries (Baltimore: The Johns Hopkins Press,
1963).
[2]The number and variety of feminist utopian novels
written in the last decade is interesting in itself.
In a recent article I identify ten of these novels and
discuss, in terms of the utopian genre, their
innovations in both form and content. Among these
novels art, or the creative process, is clearly
important in Dorothy Bryant's *The Kin of Ata are Waiting
for You*, Ursula LeGuin's *The Dispossessed*, Doris
Lessing's *Canopus in Argos: Archives*, Marge Piercy's
Woman on the Edge of Time, Mary Staton's *From the Legend
of Biel*, and Monique Wittig's *Les Guerillieres*. For

meals, and some aesthetic pleasure may be derived from the elaborate feathered garments worn by priests, such references are the extent of allusions to art in More's pace-setting work. Similarly, in the utopian novels of the nineteenth century, almost no serious attention is given to the major forms of art. For example, in an important and typical work of the period, Edward Bellamy's *Looking Backward*, technology fascinates the characters far more than the aesthetic. Although Julian West listens to symphonies, he does so via the new technological wonder -- the radio -- which, Dr. Leete assures him, provides much more pleasure than live concerts.[4]

Interestingly, then, it is only in recent feminist utopian fiction that serious attention to art and a celebration of its function have become part of the genre. In general, these novels by women seem to value creativity for its relation to the development of individual self-expression, and aesthetic pleasure for its recreative qualities. This attention to and encouragement of the arts in most feminist utopian fiction is certainly striking, but even more fascinating is Doris Lessing's subtle exploration of the function of art in her recent

----

additional discussion of these books see Lee Cullen Khanna, "Women's World's: New Directions in Utopian Fiction," *Alternative Futures: The Journal of Utopian Studies* 4 (Spring/Summer, 1981), 47-60.

[3]This attitude towards art pervades the *Republic*, and the following Socratic statement from Book III is thus typical: "It seems then that if a man who in his cleverness can become many persons and imitate all things should arrive in our city and want to give a performance of his poems, we should bow down before him as being holy, wondrous, and sweet, but we should tell him that there is no such man in our city and that it is not lawful that there should be. We would pour myrrh on his head and crown him with wreaths, and send him away to another city. We ourselves would employ a more austere and less pleasure-giving poet and story-teller for our own good, one who would imitate the speech of a good man and would express himself in accordance with the patterns we laid down when we first undertook the education of our soldiers" (*Plato's*

utopian novels, *Canopus in Argos: Archives*. In fact, the relationships between art and truth, art and the well-being of the social order, and between the artist and his work all become crucial in Lessing's *Marriages between Zones Three, Four and Five*. Although "song" is important in the entire *Canopus* series, the second novel, *Marriages*, can deal more fully with the issue of art, because its narrator is, in fact, a "singer."

Ostensibly the narrator's focus is the story of Al•Ith, the beautiful queen of Zone Three -- a delightful feminist utopia. But the telling gradually becomes as important as the facts of Al•Ith's adventure. Those facts can, indeed, be summarized quite simply. At the beginning of the book, Al•Ith is ordered, the narrator tells us, to marry Ben Ata, the king of the militaristic and despised lower world, Zone Four. These orders come from "the Providers" who remain mysterious superior figures whose authority is never questioned. In the course of the novel, Al•Ith learns to love Ben Ata and teaches him much about the nature of women and, indeed, the responsibility of a kingdom. She herself, however, suffers from this love by experiencing a possessiveness and jealousy she had never known in Zone Three, and, at last, by losing the

----

Republic, ed. G. M. A. Grube [Indianapolis: Hackett Publishing Co., 1974], p. 68.) In Book IV Socrates cautions against innovations in song or poetry: "one should be cautious in adopting a new kind of poetry and music, for this endangers the whole system. The ways of poetry and music are not changed anywhere without change in the most important laws of a city . . . it is here in music and the arts, that our guardians must build their bulwark against change" (*Plato's Republic*, p. 90). This evaluation of both art and change is diametrically opposed to Doris Lessing's, as the rest of my paper should make clear.

[4]The transformation of social, economic and political systems competes with technology as a major interest in most nineteenth-century utopian fiction. Probably the major exception to the general neglect of the arts in these novels is the attention to craftsmanship in William Morris's *News from Nowhere* As an artisan himself, Morris incorporates a love of beautiful things into his rural utopian world; there fine furnishings,

husband and son she has come to care about so terribly.
Her ultimate fate seems to be alienation from both
worlds, with only the suggestion of some mysterious
ascent to Zone Two to compensate for her very real
pain. But the novel is paradoxical in more ways than
one: the once happy Al•Ith must lose her autonomy in
order to grow; the peaceful and pleasure-loving utopian
world of Zone Three must experience discontent and
preparation for war in order to stay vital, and,
finally, the reader's attachment to Al•Ith and Ben Ata
must yield to the realization that it is the song
itself, the tale of Al•Ith that matters most.

The importance of song is suggested at the outset
of the novel, which, in fact, begins in a somewhat
surprising way:

> Rumors are the begetters of gossip. Even
> more are they the begetters of song. We,
> the Chroniclers and song-makers of our
> Zone, aver that before the partners in
> this exemplary marriage were awake to what
> the new directives meant for both of them,
> the songs were with us, and were being
> amplified and developed from one end of
> Zone Three to the other.[5]

Thus is "song" or art clearly established as the major
concern in the utopian world of Zone Three. Despite
this respect for art, however, the utopian citizens do
not know what verses are being sung in the lower world
of Zone Four. One of the accomplishments of the
narrator's tale is the major shift in aesthetic
awareness that occurs by the end of the novel. The
music, the art of all Zones becomes readily available
to everyone. In fact the fable concludes in the
following way:

----

woodworking, jewelry, colorful costumes, and graceful
objets d'arts abound. Yet even in Morris's appealing
utopia, the function of art is limited to the
decorative.

[5]Doris Lessing, *The Marriages Between Zones Three, Four,
and Five* (New York: Alfred A. Knopf, 1980), p. 3. All
subsequent references to the novel will be cited from
this edition and documented in the text.

> There was a continuous movement now, from
> Zone Five to Zone Four. And from Zone
> Four to Zone Three -- and from us, up the
> pass. There was a lightness, a freshness,
> and an enquiry and a remaking and an
> inspiration where there had been only
> stagnation. And closed frontiers. For
> this is how we all see it now. The
> movement is not all one way -- not by any
> means. For instance, our songs and tales
> are not only known in the watery realm
> "down there" -- just as theirs are to us
> -- but are told and sung in the sandy
> camps and around the desert fires of Zone
> Five (p. 245).

The reversal of attitude represented by the free
movement of song is achieved through Al•Ith's decent
and suffering -- but only when it is rightly understood
through the power of art. The fact that Lessing
presents the story of Al•Ith through the perspective of
an artist allows her to trace the relationship between
creator and work in ways that illuminate both -- and
the reader as well.

At first, the reader, like the narrator, assumes
the superiority of Zone Three and is shocked at the
impending marriage, grieves as Al•Ith dresses in dark
blue to confront the brutish soldiers come to fetch
her, and feels only loss as she crosses the border to
Zone Four. At first, as well, the reader is rather
entranced by the special claims to truth advanced by
the narrator as he tells the story of Al•Ith. For the
narrative voice, although established as one of a group
of Zone Three chroniclers, distinguishes itself by
noting the lack of accuracy in other versions of the
story. For example, early in the novel, the narrator
says:

> Our Chroniclers and artists have made a
> great thing of this exchange between
> Al•Ith and the soldiers. Some of the
> tales begin at this point. She is erect
> before them, on her horse, who hangs his
> head, because of the long difficult ride.
> She is soothing it with her white hand,
> which glitters with jewels . . . *but*

> *Al Ith was known for her simple dress, her*
> *absence of jewels and splendor!* . . . All
> kinds of little animals have crept into
> this picture. . . . Some tales tell how
> the soldiers try to catch the birds and
> the deer, and are rebuked by Al•Ith.
> *I take the liberty to doubting whether the*
> *actual occasion impressed itself so dramatically on*
> *the soldiers, or even on Al Ith* (italics mine;
> pp. 9-10).

The narrator's claims to special truth seem designed
simply to enhance his credibility, but gradually the
comments about his relation to artistic tradition vary,
and begin to engage the reader in speculations about
the truths of art.

For example, about half-way through the text,
instead of remarking that other artists have shown this
scene differently -- and he knows better -- the
narrator, recently identified as Lusik, acknowledges a
special truth in art. The moment described is the
exchange between the troubled Al•Ith and her former
lover/friend, Kunzor. He advises his queen to accept
her alienation from her past self and from her Zone.
"Al•Ith," he says, "you know there is nothing you can
do." The narrator continues:

> Soon the sky lost its light, and became a
> soft grape color, and the winds from the
> east began rustling the grasses. The two
> horses stepped down carefully till they
> were close to the stream and sheltered
> from it. And the girl and the man sat
> close, holding hands, deep in trouble,
> sustaining each other.
> When this scene is portrayed, the two
> are always shown sitting apart from each
> other, not touching . . . *And I think that*
> *this is the truth of how it was* (italics mine;
> p. 113).

The narrator goes on to say that Kunzor did hold
Al•Ith's hand through the long night, but, in spirit,
they were apart as the artists have portrayed. The
confidence that his own version of the tale is somehow
truer than other renderings seems to have faded -- as
indeed Al•Ith's confidence in herself has. A little

Lee Cullen Khanna

later in the text, the narrator comments on the
inadequacy of the much-heralded song festival in Zone
Three, noting that the songs of the women of Zone Four
were much more efficacious. His, his society's, and
the reader's confidence in the superiority of Zone
Three is beginning to ebb.

This change in attitude, advanced through a change
in attitude towards art, is carried further later, when
the narrator describes the ceremonial parade of Ben Ata
and Al•Ith through Zone Four, after she has become
pregnant. "I do not believe," Lusik says, "that any of
our artists, or our ballad-makers or songsters, have
got anywhere near the truth of that scene. And in fact
perhaps those Zone Four pictures that have the child
already born and sometimes even on his own little horse
riding in front of both Ben Ata and Al•Ith have got
nearest to it" (p. 149). But it is only towards the
end of the story -- after Al•Ith has received the
devastating news that she must leave her husband and
child and that Ben Ata will marry the queen of Zone
Five -- that the narrator calls attention to a famous
"scene" of the tale without qualification.

> Through the long dark night goes Al•Ith,
> seeing the gleam of the canals beside her,
> the white shimmer of the peaks of Zone
> Three ahead. Her horse is slow and
> careful under her. And all night the
> tears run down her face. *So she is
> pictured. And so she was* (Italics mine; p.
> 188).

At this moment art and life coincide perfectly.

Later, long after Al•Ith has returned to Zone
Three, Lusik again observes a discrepancy between
paintings of Al•Ith and the facts of her life. Although
one of the most popular pictures is of Al•Ith riding
down to Zone Four, Lusik says, "the fact is that Al•Ith
did not return to Zone Four" (p. 227). In the
painting, too, she rides her beloved horse, Yori, but
Yori had died after her final exile to Zone Three. Yet
the narrator no longer claims distinction for his
awareness of reality. Instead he says, "it is
necessary, it is forgivable in us, the songsters and
the Chroniclers and the portrayers, when we soften
certain facts" (p. 227). And, although he does not say
so explicitly, the reader can hardly avoid the

impression that artistic renderings of Al•Ith's tale
are, in some sense, truer than the actual events. The
beloved horse, Yori, cannot die; Al•Ith will forever
ride down into Zone Four. Such is the power of art to
immortalize and to transform suffering into joy.

A further example of art's superiority to literal
fact is the narrator's intriguing allusion to Dabeeb,
Al•Ith's closest female friend in Zone Four. Dabeeb
visits the exiled queen and the narrator says: "Another
figure that has never achieved realism is Dabeeb, who
is shown most often as a singer, as if this were her
profession" (p. 227). But he does not go on to say
what the reader knows, that Dabeeb was not a singer by
profession. On the contrary, it is her singing he next
speaks of, for "in the early morning, when most of the
women had fallen asleep, and Al•Ith was dozing, curled
in the grasses, Dabeeb, who was too sad to sleep, was
singing quietly to herself" (p. 227). Since the song
she sings restores Al•Ith by enabling her to embrace
her suffering as a positive force, the artistic
rendering of Dabeeb as a singer is truthful in terms of
her most essential function in the tale. The narrator
thus testifies tacitly to the superiority of art.

But Lessing will allow no stasis. Still later in
the tale, Lusik qualifies the truth of a "scene" about
Murti•, Al•Ith's sister. Murti• is now queen and
threatened by Al•Ith's grief and the new attitudes it
brings into the once joyous Zone Three. She confronts
her sister angrily. The narrator observes:

> We have pictures of Murti•, showing her
> with a harsh and bitter face, sitting on
> her horse gazing down from that height at
> poor Al•Ith, the outcast among her humble
> beasts.
> Well, it certainly happened, and is
> honestly recorded as far as it goes. But
> I for one have brooded often enough on the
> scene . . . and I believe that if we were
> able to know what she undergoes, we would
> find that she is not very distant from
> Al•Ith now, in her own way (p. 242).

In this final reference to a "scene" the
artist/narrator is shown brooding on the possible
fallibility of art. Thus Lusik has moved from pride in
his own individuality as the best singer, to

Lee Cullen Khanna

acknowledging the general superiority of the artistic
tradition in which he works, to questioning that
tradition. But now he is not arrogant. He lays no
claim to truth himself; he broods. In this brooding,
it seems to me, there is the necessary dynamic of the
true artist, one who can indeed enhance the tradition
in which he works -- because he has suffered and
matured himself.
     By the end of the story, then, the self-confidence
of the narrator has changed to a much more thoughtful
weighing of the truths of art and life. This
meditation on his art becomes explicit for Lusik after
Al•Ith has gone up to Zone Two and struggles to
understand the shapes and fires that she senses there.
In the process of trying to understand that new Zone,
she turns, as she does so often throughout the tale, to
the idea of song. She sat, says the narrator,
"dreaming of us, the song-makers, the tale-tellers,
wondered if we see what we tell . . . " (p. 197). As
he thinks of Al•Ith thinking of song-makers, Lusik
adds:

          And here I must raise my own voice, say
          something -- not on my own behalf of
          course, for there is no "I" here, "I" can
          only be the "we" of equals and colleagues.
          . . . Suppose that Al•Ith, at that moment,
          shivering with arms around her knees, and
          her head full of fiery beings not herself,
          was in fact -- and no less than any one of
          us who are supposed to be different and
          gifted and specialized -- herself a
          storyteller, ballad-maker, Chronicler;
          herself and on her own account? (p. 197).

In this speculation the protagonist of the story might
become its creator. Then Lusik continues this rather
remarkable meditation on the creative process and says:

          I am not only a Chronicler of Zone Three,
          or only partially, for I also share in
          Al•Ith's condition of being ruler insofar
          as I can write of her, describe her . . .
          and so I record here only that when Al•Ith
          sat and dreamed of Zone Two, she was Zone
          Two, even if in the most faint and distant
          way, and her imaginings of its immaculate

> fire-born beings brought her near them,
> and when she thought of us, the
> Chroniclers, she was us . . . and so now,
> in this footnote to Al•Ith's thoughts on
> that occasion, I simply make my cause and
> rest it: Al•Ith am I, and I Al•Ith, and
> everyone of us anywhere is what we think
> and imagine (p. 199).

The teller and the tale have merged; the creative act is seen to be a crucial act of life. If Descartes could say *Cogito ergo sum*, Lessing goes further to say, I create therefore I am.

The recognition that teller and tale are one and that art can even, in some sense, create life must result in a keen awareness of the dangers as well as the positive potential of imagination. For just as art can summon the marvelous images of utopia (Zone Three), so too it can summon the nightmares of human experience -- and make them real. This is the fact that so disturbed Plato. But, whereas that first utopist would banish the artist if he dared sing of anything but the rational, good, and beautiful, Lessing's singer comes to celebrate the total power of art. Lusik says:

> We Chroniclers do well to be afraid when
> we approach those parts of our histories
> (our natures) that deal with evil, the
> depraved, the benighted. Describing, we
> become. We even -- and I've seen it and
> have shuddered -- summon. The most
> innocent of poets can write of ugliness
> and forces he has done no more than
> speculate about -- and bring them into his
> life. . . . Yet there is a mystery here
> and it is not one that I understand:
> without this sting of otherness, of --
> even -- the vicious, without the terrible
> energies of the underside of health,
> sanity, sense, then nothing works or can
> work . . . the very high must be matched
> by the very low . . . and even fed by it
> (p. 198).

Thus Lessing's artist finally affirms a dialectic, the dramatic flux of life -- the necessary descent and consequent ascent symbolized by Al•Ith's marriage and ultimate movement into Zone Two. But the reader comes to see that only art can explain, facilitate, give meaning to such changes. Without the song, there is only suffering.

In the course of the novel there are many moments when Al•Ith suffers terribly, yet finds her way through song. After her initial return from Zone Four, when she is torn between the claims of the two worlds, she sings. As she, in the words of the narrator, "wandered in the between places, unknown, ignorant," she sang:

> Sorrow what is your name!
> If I knew your name I could feed you --
> Fill you, still you, and leave you! (p. 118).

Later, during her ultimate exile, "all one vast hungry ache for her Yori, and for her husband," she thought:

> A song. What I want to find is a song.
> There must be one. Songs and tales, yes they tell. They sing. Instruct . . . (p. 199).

At that point some lyrics come into her head, "I shall ride my heart thundering across the plains . . ." (p. 199). But she can get no further. It is her friend Dabeeb who supplies additional verses when she visits Al•Ith and sings:

> I shall ride my heart thundering across the plain
> Outdistance you all and leave myself behind . . .
> Sting my self-contents to hunger
> Teach me to love my hunger,
> Send me hard winds off the sands . . .(p. 228).

Hearing these lyrics, Al•Ith gets down on her knees before Dabeeb and begs for the entire song. She is told that it comes from Zone Five and responds, "That it should come from there -- there" (p. 229).

The source of the song, the lowest of the known zones, seems ironic to Al•Ith because she, and the singers and citizens of Zone Three, have so long assumed their own superiority. Similar ironies elsewhere in the tale suggest, in cumulative effect, that art should know no boundaries nor hierarchy. It is not the Zone Three song festival, for example, but that of Zone Four that proves most efficacious in restoring well-being to both worlds. And the narrator's early self-congratulation on the absence of songs of lamentation in Zone Three proves most ironic, since he himself finally chants a tale of loss and sorrow that gives meaning to Al•Ith's experience -- and instructs his entire zone. The reader eventually realizes that it was, in fact, the absence of songs of struggle, loss, and suffering that blinded Zone Three to its own limitations. In their self-satisfaction, based on genuine and remarkable achievement, they have forgotten the need to grow, test themselves, take risks, aspire. Indeed, as Al•Ith realizes after her suffering, they have totally forgotten about the existence of Zone Two. To reach that magnificent azure land above them should be the goal of their lives, but this they cannot remember until Al•Ith descends. Or rather, they cannot remember it, nor can the reader, until Lusik has sung the song of Al•Ith's descent.

In the course of the novel, then, the reader learns much about the power of art and its profound relationship to truth. The delights of aesthetic pleasure are indeed appropriate to the dream of utopia -- to the charm of Zone Three. But such delights are not sufficient, for there can be no static "good society" in Lessing's view. The dialectic of human experience is inescapable. Only through song can we hear such hard truths and turn them to good. In Lessing's dynamic utopian vision, it is art that facilitates and gives meaning to change.

OPPOSING NECESSITY AND TRUTH:
THE ARGUMENT AGAINST POLITICS IN
DORIS LESSING'S UTOPIAN VISION

Thomas I. White

A conception of the appropriate role of politics
is an essential element of utopian speculation, so we
should expect to find this topic attended to in Doris
Lessing's recent series of novels, *Canopus in Argos:*
Archives (*Shikasta*, *The Marriages Between Zones Three, Four,*
and Five, and *The Sirian Experiments*). In fact, one of
the dominant themes throughout the series is what a
great threat politics is. An important part of
Lessing's utopian vision is the thorough rejection of
the political. Lessing sees politics as an essentially
emotional enterprise, proceeding especially from pity
and pride. Consequently, it leads to the unacceptable
condition of some people running the lives of others;
and because it relies on an emotional language,
politics has no intrinsic connection with truth.
Politics thus is not only incapable of fostering but
actively prevents both the growth and evolution that is
at the center of Lessing's utopian vision.
    The most appropriate point of departure for a
discussion of Lessing's evaluation of politics is a
general outline of her utopian vision. After all,
involvement in politics is a major sign that a
particular individual or society is in a weakened
condition, so it is important to know from what
politics is such a significant departure.
    The heart of Lessing's utopian vision is
evolutionary and teleological. She posits a cosmic
Order or Harmony that should govern all human action
and natural processes, and that, when properly
observed, leads to individual, racial, generic,
planetary, and ultimately cosmic growth. This is
evident in each of the three novels. In *Shikasta* we are
told that the purpose of the Lock between the mother

planet Canopus and the developing Rohanda is to institute the latter's "Forced-Growth Phase" and this is part of furthering "the prime object and aim of the galaxy" -- "the creation of ever-evolving Sons and Daughters of the Purpose."[1] *Marriages* is a tale of the restoration of Order in the Zones by the Providers and chronicles the evolution of its main characters, Al•Ith and Ben Ata, as well as that of some of the basic features of Zones Three, Four and Five. Similarly, *The Sirian Experiments* recounts the growth of Ambien II, one of the Sirian Empire's main officials, away from a narrow Sirian viewpoint to a broader Canopean perspective. She comes to recognize the abiding Necessity and purpose of the cosmic Order and this sets the foundation for the development of a more advanced conception of Sirius's idea of its appropriate purpose as an empire. The picture we get throughout the novels is that the proper Order includes: harmony and friendship among all living beings -- between all people and between people and animals; valuing ourselves not primarily as individuals but "only insofar as we are in harmony with the plan, the phases of our evolution" (S. p. 38) (thus personal achievements or even personal survival are secondary to advancing cosmic evolution); obedience to the overall Order of things from an internal perception of its validity, not from the compulsion of external authority; the absence of private property and greed; a respectful, not wasteful, attitude towards natural resources; and a sensible planning of the shape and size of human communities -- an architecture of harmony and proportion and care about the size of the population. These are the main conditions "according to Necessity," that is, the main conditions that will foster growth.

We actually do not see much of the positive side

----

[1]Doris Lessing, *Canopus in Argos: Archives, Re: Colonized Planet 5, Shikasta* (New York: Alfred A. Knopf, 1979), 17, 35. Subsequent references to this and the other novels in the series (*The Marriages Between Zones Three, Four, and Five* [New York: Alfred A. Knopf, 1980] and *The Sirian Experiments* [New York: Alfred A. Knopf, 1981) will be made in parentheses in the body of the paper, e.g., (S. p. 15; M. p. 68; SE. p. 273).

Thomas I. White

of Lessing's utopian vision in the three novels because
they all have more to do with situations very far from
ideal. *Shikasta* tells of the crippled condition of the
planet Rohanda after it has been taken over by the dark
forces of Shammat of the evil opposing empire Puttiora.
Marriages reveals the character of the defective
condition into which Zones Three, Four and Five have
fallen. And *The Sirian Experiments* details the self-
interested and short-sighted cosmic vision of the
Sirian Empire. Yet despite the variety in the
defective states that the novels describe, there are a
number of crucial basic similarities. And focusing on
these will begin to reveal the major features of
Lessing's argument against politics.

The most succinct way of putting the essence of an
impaired, weakened or crippled state is: disobedience
to Order and Necessity. Johor writes that
"disobedience to the Master Plan was always,
everywhere, the first sign of the Degenerative
Disease," the major symptom of a falling away from
Order (S. p. 47). When Murti•, Al•Ith's sister, tries
to prevent the effects of the marriage with Zone Four
from taking hold in Zone Three, she is in effect
disobeying the will of the Providers (M. p. 118, 238).
And two of the main characters in *The Sirian Experiments*
fall because of disobedience. Shortly after meeting
Nasar, Ambien recognizes "that this was a suborned, or
disaffected, or rebellious official" (SE. p. 120).
And when Nasar warns Ambien of the danger she is in, he
says, "Sirius, rebellion is of no use, you know. That
is what you are now -- rebellion, the essence and heart
of *no, no, no* . . . . We are subject to the Necessity,
Sirius, always and everywhere. Are you thinking . . .
that you may change the Necessity itself?" (SE. p.
195-196).

Disobedience against some higher purpose requires
something lower to be put in its place, however, and
here again we see great similarities among the
instances of disobedience. For they all refuse to view
events from a larger, cosmic perspective; they all fall
away from having some appropriate purpose or function
in life that advances Order, and so they act instead
out of an absorption with the self. Johor writes that
"the very essence of the Degenerative Disease" is "to
identify with ourselves as individuals" (S. p. 38), and
"self-assertion" is one of the signs of decay in the
Giants, the race of Canopean colonists who were

assisting the Rohandan natives (S. p. 47). Similarly, the flaws keeping people trapped in Zone Six are "failure of purpose and will . . . self-indulgence and weakness" (S. p. 9).

The theme of being blind to higher purpose and, consequently, becoming self-centered is the central issue in *The Sirian Experiments*, and this underscores the importance of these concepts in Lessing's utopian vision. Sirius is an empire bereft of purpose. Reflecting on the fact that a crisis arose for Sirius when its technological development left billions of people with nothing to do but succumb to despair and then die, Ambien writes: "We had not understood that there is inherent in every creature of this galaxy a need, an imperative, towards a continual striving, or self-transcendence or purpose" (S. p. 14). Subsequently, the issue of the empire's purpose, which came to be called "the fundamental Sirian existential problem" (S. p. 63), became such a major preoccupation that by the end of the book it seems to be on the verge of leading to a revolution in the empire. Lacking any overriding purpose, however, Sirius runs its empire simply according to material self-interest and, as the Canopean Nasar puts it, "a temporary balance of social opinion -- never according to Need" (SE. p. 151). That is, not having evolved sufficiently to determine its actions according to the Necessity of cosmic harmony, all that Sirius can do is to try to forestall the pressing questions of what its proper function is by focusing on material "progress," space exploration, and colonization. And from its achievements and self-centeredness grows a pride that is yet another symptom of an impaired condition.

Ultimately, pride is the major sign of the self-centeredness that replaces an awareness of purpose. And in the same way that *The Sirian Experiments* shows the cosmic consequences of lack of purpose, so *Marriages* shows the effects of self absorption and pride on an entire Zone of reality. The Chronicler of *Marriages* tells that Zone Three's prosperity and absence of discord led to a certain pride and then to insularity. Reflecting on the introspection that followed the Providers' order that Al•Ith marry the ruler of Zone Four, Lusik writes: "And we saw how long it had been since we thought at all of what lay beyond our borders. . . . We had perhaps grown insular? Self-sufficing?" (M. p. 6). In fact, Zone Three's pride and sense of

Thomas I. White

superiority was so great that their sense of reality
effectively excluded all the other Zones. "It cannot
be said," records Lusik, "that Zone Four had for us the
secret attractions and fascinations of the forbidden:
the most accurate thing I can say is that we forgot
about it" (M. p. 4). Similarly, Al•Ith learns from her
sojourn in Zone Four that Zone Three has also forgotten
about Zone Two; again this is through self-satisfaction
and false contentment.[2] And Zone Three's pride led to
disobedience. Murti• tries to prevent Al•Ith's contact
with either Zones Four or Two from having any effect on
Zone Three. It even happens in this peaceful Zone
without a trace of militaristic heritage, that citizens
set up an army at the border to prevent anyone from
Zone Four from entering, and that a guard is placed
around Al•Ith to isolate her and so to prevent
"disorder," as Murti• puts it.

Again, we find the same thing described in the
other novels; that is, disobedience or a less developed
state can be traced to pride. Ambien writes that it
was because of "various forms of pride" that Sirius
failed to ask Canopus or even itself the critical
fundamental questions that would teach it what the
appropriate aim of their actions should be and thereby
make it possible to obey the Necessity (SE. p. 43).
The Giants who disobey the order to abandon Rohanda do
so out of pride that they know better than Canopus how
to look after the natives' welfare. And Johor records
that the condition of Taufiq, his Canopean colleague
who has been taken over by the enemy, is "an excess of
self-esteem, pride, *silliness*" (S. p. 11).

It is at this point that we can begin to see the
rationale for Lessing's critique of politics because
pride, she suggests, is one of the chief emotions that
causes politics to come into being. However, before we
look at the specific connection between pride and
politics, we should underscore that the connection is
there because pride is an emotion. That is, a central
aspect of Lessing's view of politics is that it
proceeds from emotion. This is made especially clear
in *Shikasta*, which identifies emotionalism as one of the

----

[2]The theme of "forgetting" parts of reality also
appears in *Shikasta* where Lessing talks about Britain's
having forgotten about Rhodesia (S. p. 330).

-138-

main features of Shikasta's weakened condition and
which illustrates the obsession with politics and its
highly emotional character during the planet's Last
Days. Lessing seems to be suggesting that the two feed
each other.

There are two important dimensions to the
connection between the emotions and politics. First,
the chief emotions that are at play proceed from the
great self-absorption that is a sign of being out of
phase with cosmic Order. These emotions are pride and
pity, and they manifest themselves as two of the main
weaknesses of politics -- factionalism or partiality
and a sincere desire to influence things for the good.
Second, since politics is an emotional enterprise, the
language of politics is going to be a language of
feeling, not of intellect. Propaganda, rhetoric and
slogans may sway the hearts of the masses, but they do
not uncover knowledge or inform the mind. That is,
there is no connection between the language of politics
and truth; rhetoric and slogans cannot describe and
therefore cannot advance cosmic Growth and Order.

The first way that we can see the connection
between emotions and politics, then, is through pride,
or a feeling of being better than others; and the first
manifestation of this is in the pride of the
individuals who seek positions of authority. Johor
reports that many Canopeans working on Shikasta
mistakenly succumbed to politics. He writes, "[They
believed] that they were *better than others* whose belief
in self-interest was open and expressed, better because
they, and they alone, knew how the practical affairs of
the planet should be conducted. An *emotional* reaction
to the sufferings of Shikasta," he observes, "seemed to
them a sufficient qualification for curing them" (S. p.
76; italics mine). The main example of this mistake is
Taufiq (John Brent-Oxford) who is led into politics
through pride: "It was not as simple as that he wanted
crude power, crude authority," notes Johor, "no, he
visualized himself 'influencing things for the good.'
He was an idealist: a word describing people who
described themselves as intending good, not self-
interest at the expense of others" (S. p. 76). In *The
Sirian Experiments* Ambien yields to the same temptation,
seeing herself as the only source of salvation for the
city Lelanos. Reflecting on the fact that there was a
delay in her coming to power, she writes that she was
"full of grief on behalf of Lelanos, the deprived --

the deprived of *me*, and my expert and benevolent guidance" (SE. p. 202).

Pride is also connected with politics, however, in determining the adversarial or factional character of politics. Each contestant (whether individual or interest group) in the political arena tries to advance only its welfare and, presuming its superiority to all other groups, defines its interest in total separation from and disregard for anyone else. Each group sees only its aims as worthwhile and only its answers to any problems as correct. The fact that factionalism is a sign of Shikasta's impaired condition is clear from Johor's account of the early symptoms of the Giant's falling away -- "faction-fighting, argument, and raised voices" instead of understanding obedience to Canopean Law (S. p. 47). Similarly, he says that during the planet's Last Days "what was remarkable about this particular time was how much [the people] all resembled each other, while they spent most of their energies in describing and denigrating differences that they imagined existed between them" (S. p. 78). Describing this as an essential feature of politics, Johor writes:

> Nearly all political people were incapable of thinking in terms of interaction, of cross-influences, of the various sects and "parties" forming *together* a whole, wholes -- let alone of groups of nations making up a whole. No, in entering the state of mind where "politics" was ruler, it was always to enter a crippling partiality, a condition of being blinded by the "correctness" of a certain viewpoint. And when one of these sects or "parties" got power, they nearly always behaved as if their viewpoint could be the only right one (S. p. 76-77).

Partiality and narrowness are also evident in what Sirius does, because all of its decisions about how to treat natural resources, animals used in experiments, and even the citizens of its colonies are made in terms of what will advance its own shortsighted material interests. The Sirian viewpoint is blinded by such partiality that they assume everyone else operates that way. So they continually distrust Canopus and misunderstand the point of all of its actions. And

Murti• is so wrapped up in the ways of Zone Three that all she can think of when confronted with the unrest brought on by Al•Ith's marriage to Zone Four is to preserve the peace and contentment she sees as her Zone's interest and thereby work against the common interest of the three Zones.

The second major weakness of politics, the sincere desire to influence things for the good, is also related to pride, but it comes from another emotion -- pity. The politician is genuinely moved by other people's problems and sincerely wants to alleviate them. Taufiq's altruistic desire has already been mentioned, and Ambien defends Sirian colonial rule to her Canopean tutor by appealing to "the concern we show for the good of all" and "how individual officers sacrifice themselves for their charges" (SE. p. 242). Indeed, one of Ambien's Sirian colleagues responds to her charge that the Empire might be a dictatorship by arguing: "If we are dictators, then when have there been rulers so responsive to the needs of their subjects . . . so compassionate . . . so concerned for the general good . . ." (SE. p. 272).

But the most vivid example of the connection between pity and politics is the temporary fall of Ambien II. Ambien is seduced by what she later describes as "the temptation of easy power" (SE. p. 264), so the political character of her fall is apparent. However, what led her to join the agent of Shammat in ruling Lelanos was being "wrung continually with pity" for the city's inhabitants (SE. p. 192). The feeling is first apparent in her reaction to the Canopean's lack of response to the city's slow decay: "I found myself watching this strong old, or elderly, female, with her simple directness, her honesties, and I was seeing in them callousness, indifference to suffering, a refusal to use powers she certainly must have, as Canopus, to relieve the lot of these Rohandans" (SE. p. 192). And the emotion becomes more intense as she considers the proposition to be put in charge of Lelanos "as long as needed to restore [it] to its former balance and health. (SE. p. 201). Looking down on the community she was "full of grief on behalf of Lelanos . . . and it was as if I held them in my protection; as if I was promising them an eternal safety and well-being" (SE. p. 202). Fortunately, Ambien comes to her senses when she sees that she is being used by Shammat and understands that Lelanos's

Thomas I. White

decay is according to Necessity. But through her pity
and pride, she had succumbed to the temptation to run
the lives of these other people. These two emotions,
then, combine to create an impulse to help others and
the arrogance to think that their problems will be
solved if they let us tell them how to live their
lives. That is, *politics* is created -- the sincere
desire to help others, the certainty that our narrow
viewpoint provides all the answers, and an
extraordinary confidence in our own abilities.
    There is, however, one other very important
connection between emotion and politics, because if
politics is such an emotional enterprise, then the
language of politics must also be emotional. And so we
are shown primarily in *Shikasta* that political speech is
rich only in feeling, not in substance. We see this
during Shikasta's Last Days first in Benjamin Sherban's
account of the conference of the Youth Organizations of
the World, which began, as he put it, with "the
familiar verbal aggressions" (S. p. 246). He writes:

> Battle was joined by the Communist Youth
> Federation (European Branch, Section 44)
> for Sport and Health, with a few routine
> references to running dogs of capitalism,
> fascist hyenas, and so-called democrats.
>   A conventional, indeed modest,
> opening move.
>   It was countered by the Scandinavian
> Youth Section of the League for the Care
> of the Coasts with references to
> tyrannical enslavers, jailors of free
> thought, and perverted diverters of the
> true currents of soaring human development
> into the muddied channels of repetitive
> rhetoric . . . .
>   And now, what said the Chinese Youth
> Representatives of Peace, Freedom and True
> Liberty? . . . With earnest dedication to
> exact definition, they offered: the use
> of superstitious and archaic religious
> dogmas to enslave the masses, and the
> empty rhodomontade of bankrupt pawns of
> the antediluvian economic system (S. p.
> 246-247).

And the same emotionally loaded language is apparent in

a Chinese report on leaders of the youth movement. For
example, the description of Benjamin Sherban begins:
"What can we say about this decadent philistine whose
filth pollutes the glorious struggle transforming the
ownership of the means of production for the benefit of
all the toilers of mankind" (S. p. 263).

The problem with political language, however, is
not just that it fosters emotionalism, which leads to
pity, pride, rebellion, and the like. Rather, because
of rhetoric's emotional and self-serving character, it
has no intrinsic connection with truth. Political
language is the language of falsehood; thus, politics
is an enterprise firmly grounded in inconsistency and
unreality. Johor describes politics as "one of the
strongest of the false ideas" of the Last Days (S. p.
76); lies, broken promises and other forms of
inconsistency are simply accepted as ordinary political
practice (S. p. 78-79); and Johor explains that "most
of the politicians of that time needed psychiatric
support, because of the nature of their preoccupation:
an *unreality* at the very heart of their every-day
decision-making, thinking, functioning" (S. p. 80;
italics mine). Thus, two consequences follow: first,
even when political language is not filled with jargon,
it is still unreal, empty and self-serving. In her
journal, Rachael Sherban reports that there are "Cattle
diseases. Sheep diseases. Pig diseases. Trees dying.
The Governments are saying this is not pollution as
such" (S. p. 267). But what does "not pollution as
such" mean? There is a way that the phrase makes
sense, but only if one is being extraordinarily
stipulative in using language and desires to ignore or
camouflage reality, not describe it truthfully. And
the second consequence of the falsehood of politics and
political language is that it leads to an inability to
recognize the truth even when presented with it, and
especially when it's given by politicians. This
Lessing illustrates with the memo by Tafta, Shammat's
main official on Shikasta, recounting the cases of four
heads of government who at Shammat's promptings decided
to reveal to their populations certain important
information that has been withheld from them. The
officials were either arrested, ousted from office,
killed, or ignored. "These tests," writes Tafta, "have
proved that the planet is immune to truth" (S. p. 262).

We have now reached a point where we can see why
Lessing thinks that politics is fatally flawed. For

Thomas I. White

however harmless or laudable pride, pity, or emotional
language might be on occasion, they create an
enterprise -- politics -- that works against the proper
order of things. Cosmic growth and evolution are
fostered not by telling people how to live their lives,
however sincere one's motives, but by helping them to
become autonomous. And people will not become
autonomous when subjected to the ordinary stuff of
politics -- orders or policies that proceed from the
narrow and "superior" viewpoint of those arrogant
enough to think they know best how to tell other people
how to live their lives. When Al•Ith returns from her
first visit to Zone Four she complains to Yori: "It is
a place of compulsion. . . . They can respond only if
ordered, compelled . . . . [But] not *the* Order, not
Order. But *do* this. *Do* that. They have no inner
listening to the Law" (M. p. 56). Thus, both Zone Four
and the Sirian Empire are captives of the political
impulse, seeing only the outer, not the inner. Not
recognizing the abiding Order of things, Zone Four is a
militaristic state of external orders, restrictions and
punishments. Similarly, since Sirius does not
understand Necessity or the proper function of an
empire, it *experiments* with the planets and creatures of
the universe, imposing a purpose from outside and
manipulating things to achieve its narrow, self-serving
aims. Canopus, in contrast, does not experiment, but
tries to create the conditions that will foster growth
and evolution. Its end is simply Order, Harmony,
Necessity -- the way things are supposed to be when
allowed to develop according to the imperatives of
their nature's latent potential. But so strong is the
desire for Order in the cosmos that as long as things
are not according to Necessity, there will be an
unhealthy disharmony -- Shikasta will remain diseased,
the life force of Zones Three and Four will continue to
ebb, and the Sirian "existential problem" will persist
with all of its unfortunate consequences.
    The second major weakness with politics is its
connection with falsehood. On the surface, Lessing's
message is obvious -- since political language is empty
and emotional, it cannot lead people to an
understanding of the truth. As long as one uses a
language based on the emotional falsehoods of faction,
self-interest, and self-satisfaction, one will never
see such truths as: the unity of all people; the
continuum of life; the importance of autonomy, growth,

change and development; the integrity of the natural
world; and the validity of a long term, cosmic
perspective. That is, the language of politics
inflicts a crippling poverty of the imagination on
those subject to it.

However, I think that Lessing is also advancing a
more important point about the connection between
political language and truth. That is, while one
cannot think certain ways or do certain things as long
as one is in the grip of political language, to be
enmeshed in *any* language is to be trapped in a
particular conception of the nature of reality.
Lessing seems to be arguing that *language itself*,
especially discursive language, does not have a close
enough connection with truth to be a sufficiently
strong force in advancing evolutionary growth. Ambien
II (Sirius) initially lacks the conceptual equipment to
understand Klorathy (Canopus). Whenever Klorathy
speaks of "Need" or "Necessity," Ambien hears "need"
and "necessity" (SE. p. 105). After her change of
viewpoint she explains that although Sirius heard what
Canopus said at the conference about Rohanda, it didn't
really understand what Canopus meant: "At the
Conference, being told that Canopus proposed to *develop*
the Colony 10 volunteers, to *stabilize* them, to *make use*
of their *evolution* to *advance* the Canopean Empire, what
we understood from this was no more than the sort of
development, stabilization, evolution, advance, that we
associated with our own territories" (SE. p. 10).

However, Ambien's change of viewpoint did not come
about by means of language, and Lessing seems to be
saying that such a conceptual growth *could* not come
about through language. Ambien's principal frustration
with the Canopeans Klorathy and Nasar is that they do
not explain enough to her. And since the kind of
discursive, explanatory language desired by Ambien is
simply the instrument for a particular mode of thought,
Lessing is ultimately arguing that a correct
understanding of cosmic Order cannot be reached through
discursive, analytical thought. Only living through a
set of experiences will bring about the appropriate
conceptual growth and consequent higher understanding.
We see the beginnings of this theme in *Shikasta* when
Lessing describes episodes of people absorbing a truth
that transcends language (Rachel's description of
conversations between George and Hasan and Benjamin's
account of the "Friendship Tutorial"), but the idea is

-145-

Thomas I. White

more evident in the second and third books of the series. During their first time together, Ben Ata says to Al•Ith: "Why don't [the Providers] tell us what is wrong, quite simply, and be done with it. And then we could put it right." But she replies: "That's not how things work -- I think that must be it" (M. p. 42). Thus, *Marriages* chronicles the effect of the two rulers on each other and the subsequent change in viewpoint, and *The Sirian Experiments* details the process that Ambien passed through in gradually acquiring a Canopean perspective.

But if language in general is insufficient for communicating ultimate truth, why does Lessing focus so much on *political* language? Why is politics such a special threat? Because politics deliberately tries to put into language what Lessing sees as transcending language, and what answers it gives take the listener in precisely the wrong direction. It is for the same reason, by the way, that religion is treated so harshly by Lessing. After all, religion and politics are the two main enterprises that claim to know the nature of reality and the best way to live and that try to force people into submission to some limited viewpoint. In virtually every conceivable way, then, politics will not advance growth and evolution.

But if Lessing is saying that the conventional institutions that use discursive language to tell us how to live our lives are not simply useless but harmful, does she think that one must simply wait upon Chance to create the necessary experience that will bring about the apropriate change of viewpoint? I think not. For what happens during the set of experiences to induce the growth of perspective? -- a stretching or developing of the imagination. And what use of language is not afflicted by a poverty of the imagination? An artistic use. So while Lessing sees no connection between politics and the kind of experience that fosters growth, she does affirm a connection between *art* and such experience. Lessing seems to be saying that the aesthetic experience can enrich the imagination in an appropriate way, and therefore contribute to evolutionary growth. The *Canopus in Argos* series itself is then her exemplification of this idea. It is her way of stimulating the reader's imagination and thus her attempt to nudge along the evolutionary process. In sum, the series is her ultimate testimony to the efficacy of art and the connection between art and truth.

BEYOND DEFENSIVENESS:
FEMINIST RESEARCH STRATEGIES

Daphne Patai

How a research problem is defined is of
fundamental importance not only in the overt results
that can be anticipated, but also in the ideological
implications of the work. In this essay I shall discuss
some feminist research strategies that have evolved
from my current research on utopian fiction by women.
The problem of the defensive posture, alluded to in the
title, will become evident as I proceed. By
"strategy," I mean a pattern of decisions that is
designed to attain certain objectives. It seems to me
that the objectives of feminist research, beyond the
immediate and specific contribution to knowledge of any
research project, are to challenge and ultimately
overturn restrictive traditional views of women, men,
and human society along with the social structures that
both legitimize and perpetuate these views. But in
working toward this larger objective one must be wary
of the trap of internal contradictions that
characterizes many feminist projects. In order to
clarify this, I shall describe the development of my
research on utopias, and then go on to the research
strategies that are applicable to other projects as
well.

I first began to look for utopian fiction written
by women while working on an article on women's role in
certain classics of male utopian literature. In the
secondary sources I had seen, rarely was any reference
made to utopias by women. Slowly I compiled a
bibliography of about seventy-five British and American
utopias by women, most of them from the late nineteenth
and twentieth centuries, and at that point I decided to
do a systematic study of these works. Within about a

year my bibliography had grown to 150 items,[1] and it is still constantly increasing due to the rapid production of utopias (especially feminist ones) today.

When I first came to design my current project, I defined it as a study of women's contributions to the utopian genre. I asked a series of questions such as: What are the political ideologies of utopias by women as distinct from men's utopias? Were these women aware of their female predecessors? Are there thematic and stylistic differences that bespeak a female literary imagination? Were these writers politically active in some way or were their utopias perhaps a compensation for the lack of political activity? But the major focus, which encompassed all these questions, had to do with the differences between utopias by women and utopias by men, and it can be summarized in the one question: What have utopias by women contributed to the utopian genre?

Before describing how I came to see that this question was a trap, I want to discuss the relationship between utopianism and feminism. Utopias, by definition, express a vision of a society in some significant ways dissimilar to the author's own society. Whether the new society is better or worse than the author's society is a separate question. In general, it is often observed that in the twentieth century, dystopias or anti-utopias -- visions of bad societies -- predominate, no doubt in response to the particular horrors of twentieth-century life, with mechanization, wars, and destruction of a magnitude never before known. The loss of confidence that accompanies such a reality may well explain the decrease of positive utopias in our time. But it is interesting to note that feminist utopias are ever increasing, and they are among the most interesting

----

[1] Lyman Tower Sargent's *British and American Utopian Literature 1516-1975: An Annotated Bibliography* (1979) was the single most helpful work in extending my bibliography. The first part of my own annotated bibliography of British and American utopias by women appears in *Alternative Futures* 4, No. 2-3 (Spring/Summer 1981), pp. 184-206.

fiction that is now being produced. For every Aldous
Huxley -- who after writing *Brave New World* and *Ape and
Essence* with their negative visions of the future,
wrote *Island*, a novel depicting an idyllic society
which, however, is destroyed at the novel's end -- for
every such discouraged writer there seem to be several
writers such as Marge Piercy, Joanna Russ, Doris
Lessing, or Ursula Le Guin, who see a better society as
a possibility but who understand that this means not
merely the transformation of political and economic
structures, but the transformation, also, of the most
basic social structures -- those that determine gender
identity.
      One of the things utopian literature specifically
has to contribute to feminism is the recognition of the
importance of a vision of the future. It is not that
one wants a precise and static image -- this would
necessarily be wrong: irrelevant at best, oppressive
at worst -- but some sense of the general values we
wish to see embodied *is* important. Everyone involved
in feminism is animated by some such vision: the
protest against injustice implies a vision of justice;
the satire of the present implies (even when it does
not explicitly contain) a positive pole against which
the present defects show up more clearly. Utopias
usually externalize these visions, give them shape, set
them in motion. Even when we disagree about the
details -- as indeed often happens -- the way in which
utopias estrange us from our present and thereby allow
us to see it more clearly is a continuing contribution
of utopian fiction. We are all, in one way or another,
involved in projections of our own future -- in both a
personal and a general way. Utopian fiction allows us
to try these futures out in imagination; to experience,
at least for a time, alternatives which we may not have
encountered in our present. They convey an
extraordinary sense of imaginative freedom -- this is,
for me, their fascination. Even when they seem
repetitive, I find their hold on the reader's
imagination compelling. A whole world of emotion is
conveyed to the reader through the narrative: the
writer may be animated by love, fear, hope, amusement,
rage, desperation -- always about the world in which
she or he lives. Utopian novels violate many of the
traditional features of novels -- they explore not so
much an individual consciousness as the consciousness
of an individual or group of individuals in a

particular world, a particular society, and this explicitly or implicitly calls into question our own world, our own society. It seems to me pointless to criticize utopian fiction -- as is frequently done -- for weakness in characterization, for example. Utopian literature can never pretend to be art for art's sake, even were this abstraction to exist -- a hypothesis I reject (Patai, 1978). Some consider the social preoccupation of utopias in itself a literary defect. This tells us more about the peculiar definition of the literary in our society than it does about utopias.

Feminism, today, is the most utopian project around. That is, it demands the most radical and truly revolutionary transformation of society, and it is going on in an extraordinary variety of ways. However devastating our critique of present society, it is important to be aware of its positive impetus. It is not always clearly articulated, but it is there: that sense of the potential for a different and better society, which our activity can create.

My experience with utopian fiction indicates that it has an extraordinary capacity for moving the reader to a new awareness. The major technique by which utopian fiction does this also has great potential as a feminist strategy in all areas. This technique is called defamiliarization. The term defamiliarization (or estrangement) comes from the Russian Formalist critic Victor Shklovsky, who wrote shortly before and after the Russian Revolution. In his essay "Art as Technique," Shklovsky (1965) analyzed the laws of literary existence by examining general laws of perception. Like others before him, he noticed that as peception becomes habitual, it becomes automatic. In ordinary speech or prose, for example, we can leave things half-said, half-finished, because the main characteristics are enough for us to recognize what is meant. This results in an economy of perceptive effort, but also in lack of awareness. We supply the missing pieces out of our pre-existing knowledge and perceptions, which means we respond in a routine rather than in a new way. For Shklovsky, the purpose of art is to "recover the sensation of life; it exists to make one feel things, to make the stone stony . . . to impart the sensation of things as they are perceived and not as they are known." Art achieves this by making things unfamiliar and thereby causing us to prolong our attention rather than to respond automatically. Poetry, for example, does this by its difficult and even impeded language. And the novel also, in many different ways, does this -- by the deviations from what is considered "natural," by non-causal sequences, narrative complexities, and unusual metaphors. All of these are devices for defamiliarizing, for breaking through the crust of the obvious and renewing awareness. Shklovsky's terminology was taken over by Bertolt Brecht (1964), who saw its political implications. Brecht's alienation effect in drama -- which is his version of defamiliarization -- aims at startling the audience, at going against what is considered "natural" and inevitable, and thereby arousing the audience's critical cconsciousness.

Utopian fiction, much more than other fiction, relies upon this technique of defamiliarization. For example, in a narrative situation in which a person from the old world struggles to explain what the old society was like, the shock or incomprehension of listeners, the different and jarring frames of reference -- all are ways of impressing upon the reader the strangeness and mutability of so much that we take for granted. The technique breaks through our automatic familiarity and acceptance of our own society by estranging us from it and making us view it critically. In *Unveiling a Parallel*, an utopian novel published anonymously in 1893 by two women, an earthman visits a city in Mars where total equality exists between the sexes. When he describes his own society, he is asked incredulously by his Martian friend how men managed to keep women from voting (Alice Ilgenfritz Jones and Ella Merchant [1893]). When we read this its impact is very strong, for it makes us, too, look at this detail in all its peculiarity, rather than as a well-known and accepted fact without specific cause. This seeing things in a new light is what defamiliarization is about.

One of the major ways in which defamiliarization works specifically in a great many utopian novels having to do with women -- whether feminist or anti-feminist -- is through the sex-role reversal. There are so many sex-role reversal utopias that they almost constitute a sub-genre; they were produced in abundance at the end of the last century and the beginning of this century, when women were agitating for the vote, but they continue to be produced today (for example

-152-

Esme Dodderidge [1979]). What happens in the sex-role reversal, of course, is that women dominate and men are dominated, and the author's ideology is clearly expressed, one way or another, through this vision. By some authors (women as well as men), this is considered to be a nightmare and the point of the work is that if women, for example, succeed in getting the vote, disasters will result: men will become virtual slaves to them, or civilization will be destroyed. On the other hand, writers with more enlightened views use the reversal to show us the cruelty of present society or to argue that a much better world will result when women are full participants or when women prevent men from shaping society through violence. A few examples will suffice to illustrate the impact of these reversals.

In Annie Denton Cridge's *Man's Rights*: *Or, How Would You Like It?* (1870), a woman dreams of a land where men stay at home and women rule, and she sympathizes with the oppression of men. She sees harried men housekeepers and fathers, hears their conversation and bemoans their lack of intellectual development and their excessive concern with their appearance. The dreams span a twenty-year period during which a Man's Rights movement develops, opposed at every turn by the women. The author's technique, throughout, is not to ridicule the women (as some anti-feminist works do, using the same device of reversal), but rather consistently to depict the men with great sympathy and show how their development is curtailed. Finally, in a reversal-within-the-reversal, the dreamer tells of her own society, in which men dominate women, and is greeted with total disbelief by these superior women convinced that man is intended by nature for an inferior station in life. Another such utopia, written by Vivian Cory under the pseudonym Victoria Cross (1935), is *Martha Brown, M. P., A Girl of To-Morrow*. This novel depicts the life of a successful political figure in an England in which women dominate. Although the novel ends with a traditional male appearing and capturing Martha's heart (an American with whom she flies off to the American west on the eve of becoming Prime Minister of England), nonetheless the carefully worked out reversal is very effective in increasing our awareness of the peculiarities of our own society. One of the many men in Martha's life is her husband, Jamie, who pouts and is dissatisfied with his lot. In describing his interaction with Maratha, Vivian Cory makes us aware of the more subtle ways in which the relations between men and women are determined by patterns of dominance and submission. Jamie is the one who runs to Martha's arms, lifts his head to hers for a kiss (she is of course bigger and stronger -- having chosen him, in part, for his delicacy), feels her arm encircling his waist. It is he who casts needy or resentful glances at her, who leans forward in his chair and cups his chin in his hand to catch her every word. Thus, despite the author's overt ideology, defamiliarization is such an effective technique that it makes an impact on the reader which is not easily forgotten.[2]

In the course of reading a great many utopias, I developed the habit of reversing much of what I encountered in order to see how things would look. But despite all my experience with reversal of norms, I still did not realize the way in which the basic definition of my project as a study of women's contribution to utopian fiction constituted a trap. Then, in July 1980, I read a review in the *Times Literary Supplement* of Joanna Rohrbaugh's book *Women: Psychology's Puzzle.* At a certain point the reviewers state: "What is not clear from *Psychology's Puzzle* is, if 'sex differences' are learnt and socially conditioned, whether there is anything at all that women as a sex can contribute to society or individual relationships that are particular to her sex or more accessible to it" [sic] (Peter Redegrove and Penelope Shuttle [1980]). When I read this, I automatically reversed the question and was struck at once by the absurdity of its underlying implications. It was evident that one cannot even ask such a question without positing the centrality of male experience and men's roles in the world, and the "otherness" of women. Asking such a question was a way of positing a particular view of the world in which women are eternally on the defensive,

----

[2]This subject is examined in more detail in my article "When Women Rule: Defamiliarization in the Sex-Role Reversal Utopia," *Extrapolation* 23, No. 1 (Spring 1982), pp. 56-69.

eternally the ones to be explained and justified.

A similar statement appears in a review article by Reesa M. Vaughter (1979) on literature about the psychology of women. At one point Vaughter writes: "A question frequently raised is, Will the psychology of women contribute to the psychology of human behavior, or is it a passing fad? Will the study of women, by women, for women, enhance our 'well-developed' theories in established areas of psychology?" Vaughter answers: Yes, the feminist perspective has a great deal to contribute to psychology; but the point is that she accepted the formulation of that question instead of challenging it; she accepted the premise implicit in the question. What such a question does is to separate women from the generally human and posit them as an "other" which in some way needs to be explained, justified, and/or defended. Reversing this formulation at once reveals all this: there is no way -- at least until now -- that one could ask: What does our knowledge of the psychology of men contribute to the psychology of human behavior? This question strikes us as absurd because the male, as a matter of course, is accepted as and presumed to be the norm, the authentic human being, against which the female is set as an other. The male is the representative of the species, and male behavior *is* human behavior -- or so we have been taught.

This experience of sudden "seeing" is a kind of revelation, in which what one has known abstractly now comes to life with special force and immediacy and, therefore, in the most fundamental sense, alters one's apprehension of "reality." Such a revelation implies a transition from passive perception to active participation, from theory to practice. No doubt such experiences -- in the innumerable forms that they may take -- are at the heart of much, perhaps all, feminist work. In my own case, this led me to see that the way I had defined my utopia project affirmed the paradigm of unquestioned male centrality, against which I was making the usual small protest.

I was, of course, not willing to stay in this trap; I did not want inadvertently to accept the paradigm of men's centrality and women's otherness by writing a book whose aim was to find out what women had contributed to the utopian genre. It was clear that I had accepted the "utopian genre" as some pre-existing thing defined by the works of men, and I had put myself

in the position of having to defend or explain what it
was that women had "contributed" to it. Once I decided
to reject this posture I saw that what most interested
me in the books I had been reading was the implicit
moral ideology that animates utopian fiction in
general. This is how my work went from being a study-
of-utopias-by-women to a book with the projected title
"The Moral Vision in Utopian Literature," offering a
new interpretation of utopian literature through the
study of utopian fiction by women -- without either
explaining or apologizing for or justifying my
selection.
    The point in making this argument is not that
there is something inherently wrong with saying this is
a study of works by women. The point -- and this is my
first strategy -- is to make such an identification
redundant by simply considering women typical human
beings and not arguing about it. This is also a way of
breaking through the presumption that writers are
necessarily male, which is what lies behind the
adjectival use of "women" in a phrase such as "women
writers." Others have of course noted this trap, but
have perhaps not seen that rejection of the dominant
paradigm -- simple, mere rejection -- is one way to
begin to unravel this particular definition of reality.
The argumentative stance (which I am necessarily
adopting here in explaining this process) is in essence
a weak one, resulting from the acceptance of the
defensive posture that men have imposed on women. Not
only did I decide to reject this posture, but it was
clear that the works I was studying deserved better
than this.
    In exactly the same way that no man ever felt
compelled to identify his work as having to do with
male novelists, or to consider his study of psychology
or linguistics as having to do specifically with male
phenomena, I decided that I would, in the best utopian
fashion, appropriate this right for myself. I would
write *as if* I were living in the twenty-second century,
say; as if it were in fact no longer necessary to argue
and insist that women's work deserves attention; as if
it were a foregone conclusion that women's work, like
men's work, was part and parcel of the real world, and
that one studied what interested one without any sense
of lesser or greater importance derived from a
polarization along gender lines. By imaginatively
casting myself into this utopian future and doing a

study in this way, I could help bring this state of affairs about.

If this seems like concealment of some type, if you would ask: how can I avoid saying that my work is specifically about women? -- then my reply is that you are accepting the tyranny of the label of otherness applied by men to women, that you are viewing the essential characteristic of such a study as being the sexual identity of the individuals whose work is being examined. It seemed to me that by making the term women synonymous with the generally human, I could avoid affirming and being trapped by the current paradigm of male centrality. By adopting this strategy of, in a sense, universalizing women, one rejects the label of otherness which always consists of seeing everything done by women in terms of femaleness. To write a book about nineteenth century fiction, say, without using the label of women, and to do this without apology or announcement, *is* to challenge the categories imposed by men. Instead of arguing, we should simply inaugurate the new approach and posit the female as the generally human. This is the first strategy I want to propose, and of course it attacks the very idea that men constitute the human norm.

An awareness of the problem of labels has inevitably accompanied the development of Women's Studies as an academic field. Women's Studies needs to exist because men have the whole university. Yet while performing a vital function within the university, "Women's Studies" cannot help but confirm the paradigm of male centrality. Since we live in the real world, however, and not yet in the twenty-second century into which I can occasionally launch myself, it is important both to support Women's Studies programs and to aim at making them redundant. In the short term, we might press for Men's Studies programs, in order to reduce the male pervasion of academic disciplines, because what is for women an expansion would be for men a reduction or restriction, and it needs to be done as well. Men's Studies programs would carry the current questioning of the dominant paradigm further, in that they would help us to see that what men have done (which generally passes for the human) is in fact influenced by and representative of the male gender role -- a socially assigned identity. This relates to my second strategy, which will be discussed below. Women's Studies, much to its credit, clearly breaks through the not-so-neat boundaries of academic categories. It seems to exist at some intersection of the sexual and the political. Yet, given the structure of the university, Women's Studies cannot help but be vulnerable to the compartmentalization that can make it appear to be a small and highly specialized area. This is a rather remarkable way of reducing women, of once again putting us in our place by signalling that all those interested in other specializations -- and not in Women's Studies--can safely ignore it. "Human Studies" is too broad a label. So is Women's Studies. If it were not reductive, it could not exist.

Women's Studies programs began by excavating women's past and exploring our present, and have progressed to a questioning of the kinds of paradigms that make a program such as Women's Studies not only necessary, but vitally necessary in universities today. As Women's Studies programs continue in the task of restructuring consciousness, they nonetheless reflect the tensions of a contradiction, for the label by gender is, in our time, still reductive. "Women" are not a subject, and can only be taken as a subject from within the very paradigm that Women's Studies programs aim to challenge and protest against -- the paradigm that expresses men's activities in terms of hundreds of specific areas all of which together add up to a rich and multifaceted reality. According to this paradigm, in opposition to this reality stand women, set off above all by our conditioned awareness of femaleness. Women's Studies, unmatched by Men's Studies, plays to this type of dichotomy.

The way in which the labelling or setting apart of women's activities is reductive is evident in many other areas. For example, *The New York Times* (like most newspapers) features photographs of men in the news and articles about men in the news, and photographs and drawings of women primarily in the advertisements. The *Times* has made a few so-called advances and one of them has been to rename its women's page the "Style" page. But on the Style page the *Times* prints all kinds of articles about women's political activities, about women scientists, and, of course, about fashion and beauty. In other words, for *The New York Times*, the main thing that has to be said about any type of political or intellectual or other endeavor in which a woman is involved is that it is a woman who is involved. For the *Times*, virtually anything

relating to women belongs on the Style page. The
implicit opposition between style and substance is
clear. More recently the *Times* has begun to carry a
column called "Hers," which is not matched by any
column called "His." This means, that men still, in
effect, have the whole newspaper while women have the
Style page and the Hers column. The Hers column is
written by women and deals with varied subjects -- but
the heading never relates to the specific subject each
time. Rather, it merely bears the sex-marked word
"Hers," which tells us nothing about the content of the
column. All these practices reaffirm the paradigm of
women's otherness at the very same time that they
purport to act as correctives. This is the
contradiction found also at the heart of much
contemporary feminism, and it must be transcended.

The first strategy that I have been discussing is,
therefore, to reject the dominant paradigm and to posit
the importance of the work done by women by refusing to
make a special point of the gender of the agents. This
means acting as if it is assumed that the subject is of
general human interest and that women constitute the
human norm. In practice, it means carefully defining
research projects in such a way that one does not
automatically fall into a defensive posture.
Especially the word "women" should be made redundant in
book titles. Elaine Showalter's book *A Literature of
Their Own* (1977), for example, could just as well have
carried the subtitle "British novelists from Bronte to
Lessing," rather than what it actually says: "British
women novelists from Brontë to Lessing." Refusing the
label of "women," because we reject the implications of
its use at this stage of history, is the first
strategy. I can state this more positively by saying
that we should try to write *as if* women, rather than
men, were the model for the human norm. This is, after
all, a long overdue corrective device. Let us assume
the interest and importance of everything related to
women, rather than eternally argue in terms which
necessarily undermine our very objectives (because the
game, of course, is rigged).[3]

----

[3]Such a strategy of course carries implications for the
marketing of books. I recognize that there is a
practical problem here, but the convenience of a

The second strategy is, in a sense, the reverse of the first. We should start to treat the many areas of research that involve men and men's activities in terms of men's gender identity, that is, of male social roles and traits. We should withdraw from men's activities and men's work our agreement (which, in fact, was never solicited) that they represent the generally human. We must cease to accept the male as the human norm, cease to omit mention of the influence of male gender identity on the many areas that it in fact influences. How do we do this? Fascinating research is being done in all areas that is contributing to such a redefinition of reality. Work on sex roles, for example, on gender identity, on parenting, on language, and on political science is now appearing that exemplifies such an approach. In the case of literary research too, works by male writers should be viewed as vehicles for the expression of a male gender identity, and this should be examined in all its variety. These works could not be anything but this, of course, yet it is seldom attended to. Some steps have been taken in this direction -- but they have usually been confined specifically to the attitudes of male writers toward women and sexuality. But male gender identity is not merely an orientation toward women or sex; it has everything to do with the political climate in which we live today, and it permeates all fields that have been defined and dominated by men.

The word "male" ought to appear in many titles in which it does not appear. For example, Frank and Fritzie Manuel (1979), in their huge book *Utopian Thought in the Western World*, virtually totally disregard

----

section labelled "Women" in a bookstore or a catalogue is a direct reflection of the smallness of these sections; were this not so, many other, non-gender, labels would be required. As in Women's Studies, here too the aim must clearly be to transform a pre-existing practice. If separatism is a necessary stage, we should nonetheless remember that separate-but-equal has never achieved true equality because of the problem of who is excluding whom. As far as intellectual work is concerned, each scholar will have to decide how her work is to be defined, pursued, packaged, and marketed; to the extent that these are within her control.

utopias by women.   In an immense index almost no woman
appears except in the capacity of wife, mother, or
sister of some man.   The Manuels' book, of course,
should have been called "Male Utopian Thought in the
Western World," given its exclusion of women.   This is,
in fact, typical.   The masculine ideology embodied in
so much of the work in the humanities -- not to mention
other fields--needs to become the focus of criticism.
George Mosse (1964), for example, in his book *The Crisis
of German Ideology*, has no listing in his index for men
or males or masculinity -- perhaps because these terms
are redundant in the study of fascism.   He does have
"women" listed, and gives four different page
references to them -- in a work of over 300 pages.   On
one of the pages that refers to women, he discusses the
analogy between the female and the Jew in the thinking
of such pre-fascist writers as Otto Weininger, but
Mosse misses the point that fascism *is* the ideology of
hypertrophied masculinity.   He has written an entire
book in which, because he believes that what men do and
think and write is in some sense the human norm, he
misses the opportunity to look at this important
historical phenomenon as being the expression of a
specific male gender identity (in my view in a
particular state of pathology; hence my use of the term
"hypertrophied masculinity").   Some scholars,
fortunately, have begun to do this and there is a
fascinating book edited by Maria Macciocchi, which
makes the connection between fascism, androcentrism,
and anti-feminism (Macciocchi, 1978).   Much more and
broader research on this needs to be done.   To give
another example, Jonah Raskin (1971) wrote a book
called *The Mythology of Imperialism* (another book dealing
only with male writers, a fact the author thought
unnecessary to mention).   Yet Raskin never discusses
imperialism as a specifically male ideology, never
mentions the convergence between imperialism and a so-
called normal male gender identity in terms of the
assumption of superiority, centrality, and domination
-- all of which require an inferiorized opposing pole.
Once again, he takes the imperialism that he discusses
(though he protests against it) as a general *human*
phenomenon.
     A third example: Steven Marcus (1966), in his
famous study of sexuality and pornography in nineteenth
century England, *The Other Victorians*, concludes that
pornography corresponds to fantasies of infantile

sexual life. In the last paragraph of his book, Marcus says that every man and every society must pass through such a phase. He does not stop to consider that man here clearly means "male," nor does he hesitate before linking the specific concerns of some males with the general concerns of every "society." This link presumes both pornography and male ascendancy as unquestioned features of life. One final example: Ashley Montagu (1976), in a book called *The Nature of Human Aggression,* argues convincingly that human aggression is learned and not innate. He criticizes the simplistic ideology that "man" is the most aggressive creature on earth and points out that only some men in some cultures are. But nowhere does he call attention to the fact that even within the very societies used as models of aggression a large group of human beings -- that is, women -- generally does not behave in this way. It is instructive, as others have no doubt noted, that even a scholar such as Montagu, in many respects a feminist, automatically falls into the assumption that the male is the norm. He could have strengthened his argument considerably by pointing out that women in our society, who are also human, are not generally violent; he could have pointed out that proponents of the aggression-is-innate view seldom deal with women. By identifying specifically male behavior patterns with some abstract human norm, Montagu misses seeing that even our society offers more than one pattern of behavior and he avoids examining what is specific about our society that encourages aggression in males. Fortunately, however, feminist scholars are working on this subject (see Stockard and Johnson [1979] for a review of this literature).

If even in these more or less obvious cases that one would have thought would evoke an awareness of male activity, male values and attitudes, no such analysis is forthcoming, what about all those other areas in which male gender ideology plays a more subtle role? The human norm which is identified with male gender identity is beginning to look more and more like an abnorm, and a very dangerous one at that.

The two strategies I have suggested, are, of course, different in nature. The first, the universalizing of women's experiences and work, without apology, is what we would find in a utopian world. So it is more than a strategy; it is an inkling of the kind of permanent change that we need. But the second strategy is much more clearly a polemical device. The strategy of viewing everything done by men as specific productions of specific males within a specific culture is meant to act as a corrective, as a reversal that also increases our awareness of what men habitually do to women, which we too internalize. But at the same time this strategy is seriously intended to allow criticisms to be made that need to be made but that cannot be articulated while the male is considered to be the model for the human species. By naming certain things as peculiarly male concerns -- for example domination and aggression as styles of behavior -- we are beginning to question their legitimacy. We need to do this, to break the identification of that-which-is-male with that-which-is-necessarily-and-inevitably-human. This is a myth, in the sense of a belief that legitimizes certain ways of doing things, that makes them look natural and inevitable and thus does not allow the practice so protected to be subject to our scrutiny.

There are a number of consequences to no longer seeing the male as the human norm or model. The first obvious result, of course, is to allow us to see the bias against women in much of the work produced by men in all fields. But there is still a further implication to a radical questioning of the male norm. One can begin to separate the generally human from the merely male. One can begin to do a critical analysis of the distortions in our knowledge as a result of the fundamental division of the world into a male center and a female periphery. In the field of political science, for example, Susan Bourque and Jean Grossholtz (1974), in an article called "Politics an Unnatural Practice," discuss the distortion that occurs when the very definition of politics is restricted, as it now is, to typicaly masculine activities. Many political scientists have considered women's concerns, when they differ from men's, to be apolitical. Politics is assumed to embody aggressive behavior, and women are defined as political only when they behave more like men -- that is, when they express enthusiasm for war, controversy, and electoral manipulation. This is the kind of radical questioning of a given reality that can result from seeing men's activities in the world, and definition of the world, as the expression of a male gender identity. Susan Moller Okin (1979), in her recent book *Women in Western Political Thought*, is also

DAPHNE PATAI

working along these lines. Of course, her book should
have been called "Women in Western Political Male
Thought."
     Ursula Le Guin raises a fundamental issue in her
book *The Left Hand of Darkness* (1969) when she asks what
kind of institutions might have developed in a society
in which gender identity and sex roles were not the
primary fact of life that they are made to be in our
society. In the field of literary criticism, and
perhaps in all our work, our language is often based on
a model of domination and control: we want to master a
subject, to penetrate a problem, to break the back of a
dilemma. Writing is full of this type of vocabulary.
We seem to view our work as standing in some sort of
opposition to us which we must overcome. We conquer
and tame the problem or object of study. But is there
anything "natural" about this language -- or is it
telling us something important about the way we have
learned to construe our activities? Are not there
other intellectual models available? Nowhere is this
vocabulary more frightening and dangerous than in the
political arena. The boys in Washington provide a
telling example of how supposedly political problems
are couched in the language of male dominance and
aggression. Can we hope to avoid nuclear war long
enough to bring about a questioning of the desirability
of these male norms? The macho political style needs
to be exposed as the sclerosis of the male gender role
that it is.

     In my research on utopian fiction I have not found
or even heard of a single utopia by a man that posited
a society composed entirely of men. But there are
quite a few feminist utopias in which societies
composed exclusively of women are envisioned. However
we expain the difference between male and female
behavior in our society today, there are real
differences in that behavior. It is not surprising, in
view of this, that women have envisioned societies
without men, while men have not envisioned the
reverse. The men would be giving up domination of a
ready-made group of victims, a domination that cuts
across racial and economic lines; while the women, in
envisioning a society without men, are merely giving up
their roles of victims and becoming persons. Utopias
by women -- radically feminist, even separatist,

-164-

utopias -- seem to recognize the danger of the aggressive/dominant male gender role to human society, and it is in response to the oppression and despair created by these roles that their alternative societies are envisioned. These societies are typically cooperative, creative, and non-aggressive in the sense that aggression is not a normal means for validating one's worth, as it is for men in our society. By contrast, even in the most enlightened of the men's utopias -- such as William Morris' *News From Nowhere* (1890) -- one finds that the authors' imaginations faltered when it came to envisioning women's place in these utopias. Although supposedly egalitarian and nonsexist, these utopias regularly reveal a rather conventional division of labor and power and the male is still assumed to be the model and measure of all things. Hence the title of my article some years ago: "Utopia for Whom?" (Patai [1974]). It is obviously very hard for male writers to break out of the comforting stereotype -- and easier for women since they are the ones who suffer from these views.

I want, finally, to express my two research strategies in a somewhat different form, using some very helpful terminology that I am borrowing from a book by Erving Goffman (1961) called *Encounters.* Goffman is always a fascinating writer, because he studies the obvious, and it is above all the obvious that needs analyzing, and that-which-goes-without-ssying that needs to be perceived.
    In this book Goffman has a long essay, "Fun in Games," in which he analyzes the personal interactions that occur in game-like situations that he calls encounters. In describing these games, Goffman refers to the way in which certain things are filtered out of our awareness while we are absorbed in the situation of playing a game. This is due to the operation of rules of irrelevance or inhibitory rules. A simple example of a rule of irrelevance is, in a chess game, the lack of attention to the value or beauty of the chess pieces. A more important example, that Goffman does not give, is our lack of awareness that the queen, as the most powerful figure in chess, with the greatest freedom of action, constitutes a reversal of our real-world norms. A rule of irrelevance governs our awareness and inhibits attention to this feature of the

DAPHNE PATAI

game. Goffman also identifies rules of relevance, which he also calls facilitating rules. These are rules that tell participants what they may attend to, what features from the world outside the game may legitimately enter their awareness. An example which is important because it gets into the area of social roles is of a person popping into the drawing room and asking "Anyone for tennis?" Goffman comments that it is not known that any servant present in the room has ever mistaken himself for "anyone." Thus social hierarchy has been preserved or attended to. These different transformation rules together create the meaning of the encounter, they provide the definition of the situation. Goffman recognizes that the game is a kind of microcosm, and that what he writes has important applications to other social settings.

Goffman's terminology is helpful to us in understanding how it is that the paradigm of male centrality and female otherness functions. It seems to me that among the major rules that prevail in society today is that men's maleness is irrelevant to most encounters, while women's femaleness follows a rule of relevance. Beyond the simple assumption of male supremacy, men's gender is simply not attended to -- it obeys a rule of irrelevance. This is why men are taken as persons, as the model of the human, and why "man" is supposed to be, even today, a sexually unmarked word. For women, however, the opposite rule holds, and we learn that we must above all recognize that the activities engaged in by women are defined by their gender. In other words, for women there is a facilitating rule that makes their gender of relevance in every conceivable situation in which they are involved. It is this that allows the *New York Times* to have a Style page on which all kinds of activities engaged in by women are jumbled together.

We can modify Goffman's terminology somewhat by recognizing that this particular rule of relevance not only facilitates but actually *demands* our awareness of the femaleness of women. A simple example suffices: we always notice women's sexual attractiveness, whether a woman is a musician or a politician. But sexual attractiveness in men need only come up for consideration in situations in which it is relevant -- for example, when a man plays the role of a lover. There are a great many roles for men in our world in which sexual attractiveness as such is irrelevant, and

-166-

very few such roles for women. When women age and no longer conform to the prevailing standard of desirability-to-men, we do not become more human; we are merely beyond the pale. It seems that as women in fact participate in more and more activities, this same rule of relevance still hounds us, so that we are forever viewed above all as women. This may be one reason why men seem to "naturally" fit most of the roles they assume, whereas women are felt to be playing a role. Goffman mentions this in another of his books, called *Gender Advertisements* (1979), and points out that even in advertising a man is habitually taken as an individual authentically engaged in some particular activity, whereas a woman appears to be a costumed female involved in a performance. It may be this rule of relevance that makes us see women above all as playing roles, as constantly on display. Certainly this is a factor in the difficulties, for women, of developing an authentic sense of self. We too learn the rules that allow men to pass as general human agents and that define our "otherness." I think it is not only that women internalize some peculiar and damaging ideas about ourselves. The ideas may change, their content may be transformed, but until the very rules of relevance and irrelevance operative in our society are questioned and overturned, we will all be trapped by the world that these rules create and that our language constantly reproduces.

My two strategies correspond to a reversal of the prevailing rules of relevance and irrelevance. I think our work and efforts will be greatly strengthened by this reversal, by applying a rule of relevance to male gender identity, and a rule of irrelevance to the femaleness of women. Perhaps in this way we can move closer to a stage in which all these rules will have ceased to apply. There are many areas of research that need to be re-examined and rethought; the possibilities are just beginning to be visible, because all research until now has been done from within a paradigm that is finally being called into question on a scale never before imagined.

When I started reading feminist utopias, I often felt discouraged because I found perfectly contemporary arguments set out in books written one hundred and two hundred years ago. It gave me the feeling that nothing had improved. But as I read more, my attitude changed. The very obscurity of the women whose work I was

DAPHNE PATAI

reading, the difficulty in many cases of finding out
anything at all about them, was a clear sign of the
perspective in which their work was placed in their own
time. This is not so today. Feminist issues have never
before reached such large groups of people -- even the
backlash against them is a token of this, and
understandable when situated historically. Feminist
research is rethinking the world and generating an
immense body of new work that is transforming our sense
of the possible and the desirable. I think that from
the perspective of some future time, it will be clear
that feminism produced the major paradigm shift of the
twentieth century.

REFERENCES

Bourque, Susan and Jean Grossholtz. 1974. "Politics an
    Unnatural Practice: Political Science Looks at
    Female Participation," *Politics and Society* 4 (2),
    225-266.
Brecht,   Bertolt.   1964.   In   John   Willett   (ed.   and
    trans.), *Brecht on Theatre*: *The Development of an
    Aesthetic*. Hill and Wang, New York.
Cridge, Annie Denton. 1870. *Man's Rights*: *Or, How Would
    You Like It?* Mrs. E.M.F. Denton, Wellesley, Mass.
Cross, Victoria (pseud. of Vivian Cory). 1935. *Martha
    Brown, M.P.,A Girl of To-morrow*. T. Werner Laurie,
    London.
Dodderidge, Esme. 1979. *The New Gulliver*. Taplinger,
    New York.
Goffman, Erving. 1961. *Encounters*: *Two Studies in the
    Sociology of Interaction*. Bobbs-Merrill, Indianapolis
    & N.Y.
Goffman, Erving. 1979. *Gender Advertisements*. Harper
    and Row, New York.
[Jones, Alice Ilgenfritz and Ella Merchant].   1893.
    Unveiling a Parallel: *A Romance*, by Two Women of the
    West. Arena Pub. Co., Boston, Mass.
Le Guin, Ursula. 1969. *The Left Hand of Darkness*.
    Walker & Co., London.
Macciocchi, Maria A., 1978. *Les Femmes et leurs maitres*.
    Christian Bourgois, Paris.
Manuel,   Frank   and   Fritzie   Manuel.   1979.   *Utopian
    Thought in the Western World*. Harvard Univ. Press
    (Belknapp Press), Cambridge, Mass.

Marcus, Steven. 1966. *The Other Victorians*. Basic Books, New York.

Montagu, Ashley. 1976. *The Nature of Human Aggression*. Oxford Univ. Press, New York.

Mosse, George. 1964. *The Crisis of German Ideology*. Grosset and Dunlap, New York.

Okin, Susan Moller. 1979. *Women in Western Political Thought*. Princeton Univ. Press, Princeton, N.J.

Patai, Daphne. 1974. "Utopia for Whom?" *Aphra* 5 (3), 2-16.

Patai, Daphne. 1978. "Context and Metacontext," *Ideologies and Literature*, 8, 3-12.

Raskin, Jonah. 1971. *The Mythology of Imperialism*. Dell, New York.

Redegrove, Peter and Penelope Shuttle. 1980. Review of Joanna Rohrbaugh's *Women: Psychology's Puzzle*. In *Times Literary Supplement*, (London), July 18.

Sargent, Lyman Tower. 1979. *British and American Utopian Literature 1516-1975: An Annotated Bibliography*. G.K. Hall, Boston.

Shklovsky, Victor. 1965. "Art as Technique," In *Russian Formalist Criticism: Four Essays*, trans. Lee T. Lemon and Marion T. Reis. Univ. of Nebraska Press, Lincoln.

Showalter, Elaine. 1977. *A Literature of Their Own: British Women Novelists from Brontë to Lessing*. Princeton Univ. Press, Princeton, N.J.

Stockard, Jean and Miriam M. Johnson. 1979. "The Social Origins of Male Dominance," *Sex Roles* 5 (2), 199-218.

Vaughter, Reesa M. 1979. "Psychology," in Juanita H. Williams (ed)., *Psychology of Women: Selected Readings*. W.W. Norton, New York. This article originally appeared in *Signs* (1976) 2 (1).

This article first appeared in *Women's Studies International Forum* 6, No. 2 (1983). I thank Pergamon Press for allowing it to appear here.

Preparation of this essay was greatly facilitated by a National Endowment for the Humanities fellowship for 1980-81.

CONTRIBUTORS

Marleen Barr, Assistant Professor of English at Virginia Polytechnic Institute and State University, is the editor of *Future Females*: (Bowling Green University Popular Press, 1981), the first critical anthology about women and science fiction. She is currently writing a book-length study of the subject for the Greenwood Press.

Nicholas D.Smith's books include *Thought Probes* (with Fred D. Miller, Jr.; Prentice-Hall, 1981) and *Philosophers Look at Science Fiction* (Nelson-Hall, 1982). Most of the essays in this volume were selected from the Sixth Annual Conference on Utopian Studies, for which he served as Program Chairperson.

Verlyn Flieger, Assistant Professor of English at the University of Maryland, teaches a course on medieval and modern literature. Her *Splintered Light*: *Myth as Meaning in Tolkien's World* will appear in Spring 1983 (Eerdmans Publishing Company).

Lucy M. Freibert, Associate Professor of English and American Studies at the University of Louisville, is currently working on a book about nineteenth-century literary figures associated with communes.

Carol Farley Kessler is Assistant Professor of English and American Studies at Penn State's Delaware County Campus. She has just completed *Elizabeth Stuart Phelps* (G.K. Hall). Her anthology *Daring to Dream*: *Utopian Fiction by United States Women Before 1920* will appear in 1983 (Routledge & Kegan Paul).

Contributors

Lee Cullen Khanna is Associate Professor of English at Montclair State College where she teaches courses in feminist utopian fiction. She is writing a book on the subject entitled *Frontiers of Imagination: Female Utopias.*

Daphne Patai teaches Brazilian literature and comparative literature at the University of Massachusetts, Amherst. Her *Myth and Ideology in Contemporary Brazilian Fiction* will appear in 1983. She is currently completing a book-length study of George Orwell and another book about contemporary Brazilian women.

Carolyn Rhodes is Professor of English and a founder of the Women's Studies program at Old Dominion University. She is the editor of *First Person Female American: A Selected and Annotated Bibliography of the Autobiographies of American Women Living After 1950* (Whitson, 1980).Professor Rhodes currently holds a Fulbright appointment in Romania.

Jewell Parker Rhodes is an Assistant Professor of English and Creative Writing at the University of Maryland. She is a 1981-1982 NEA award recipient and is currently at work on a novel.

Lyman Tower Sargent heads the Political Science department at the University of Missouri-St. Louis. He is the author of *Contemporary Political Ideologies* (5th ed. 1981), *New Left Thought* (1972), and *British and American Utopian Literature* (1979).

Thomas I. White teaches in the Philosophy and Religion department of Upsala College. Specializing in Renaissance thought, Professor White has published a number of articles on Thomas More and is currently completing a book on More's *Utopia.*